Actual Test
READING 2

Second Edition

DARAKWON

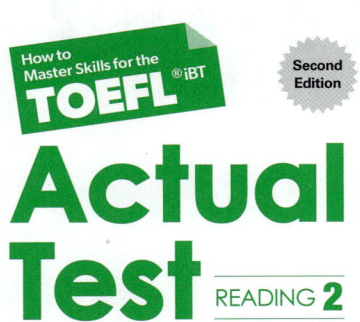

Publisher Kyudo Chung
Editor Inpyo Hong
Authors Michael A. Putlack, Stephen Poirier, Will Link
Proofreader Michael A. Putlack
Designers Minji Kim, Kyuok Chung

First Published in March 2008 By Darakwon, Inc.
Second edition first published in September 2025 by Darakwon, Inc.
Darakwon Bldg., 211, Munbal-ro, Paju-si, Gyeonggi-do 10881
Republic of Korea
Tel: 02-736-2031 (Ext. 250)
Fax: 02-732-2037

Copyright © 2008 Darakwon, 2025 Darakwon

All rights reserved. No part of this publication may be reproduced, stored in a retrieval system, or transmitted in any form or by any means, electronic, mechanical, photocopying or otherwise, without the prior consent of the copyright owner. Refund after purchase is possible only according to the company regulations. Contact the above telephone number for any inquiries. Consumer damages caused by loss, damage, etc. can be compensated according to the consumer dispute resolution standards announced by the Korea Fair Trade Commission. An incorrectly collated book will be exchanged.

ISBN 978-89-277-8109-7 14740
978-89-277-8105-9 14740 (set)

www.darakwon.co.kr

Photo Credits
Shutterstock.com

Components Main Book / Answer Key / Free MP3 Downloads
7 6 5 4 3 2 1   25 26 27 28 29

Table of Contents

Actual Test 01 009

Actual Test 02 031

Actual Test 03 051

Actual Test 04 071

Actual Test 05 091

Actual Test 06 111

Actual Test 07 131

Actual Test 08 151

Actual Test 09 171

Actual Test 10 189

INTRODUCTION

1 Information on the TOEFL® iBT

A The Format of the TOEFL® iBT

Section	Number of Questions or Tasks	Timing	Score

Reading	**20 Questions**
	• 2 reading passages
	  – with 10 questions per passage
	  – approximately 700 words long each
		35 Minutes	30 Points

Listening	**28 Questions**
	• 2 conversations
	  – 5 questions per conversation
	  – 3 minutes each
	• 3 lectures
	  – 6 questions per lecture
	  – 3-5 minutes each
		36 Minutes	30 Points

Speaking	**4 Tasks**
	• 1 independent speaking task
	  – 1 personal choice/opinion/experience
	  – preparation: 15 sec. / response: 45 sec.
	• 2 integrated speaking tasks: Read-Listen-Speak
	  – 1 campus situation topic
	    reading: 75-100 words (45 sec.)
	    conversation: 150-180 words (60-80 sec.)
	  – 1 academic course topic
	    reading: 75-100 words (50 sec.)
	    lecture: 150-220 words (60-120 sec.)
	  – preparation: 30 sec. / response: 60 sec.
	• 1 integrated speaking task: Listen-Speak
	  – 1 academic course topic
	    lecture: 230-280 words (90-120 sec.)
	  – preparation: 20 sec. / response: 60 sec.
		17 Minutes	30 Points

Writing	**2 Tasks**
	• 1 integrated writing task: Read-Listen-Write
	  – reading: 230-300 words (3 min.)
	  – lecture: 230-300 words (2 min.)
	  – a summary of 150-225 words (20 min.)
	• 1 academic discussion task
	  – a minimum 100-word essay (10 min.)
		30 Minutes	30 Points

B What Is New about the TOEFL® iBT?

- The TOEFL® iBT is delivered through the Internet in secure test centers around the world at the same time.
- It tests all four language skills and is taken in the order of Reading, Listening, Speaking, and Writing.
- The test is about 2 hours long, and all of the four test sections will be completed in one day.
- Note taking is allowed throughout the entire test, including the Reading section. At the end of the test, all notes are collected and destroyed at the test center.
- In the Listening section, one lecture may be spoken with a British or Australian accent.
- There are integrated tasks requiring test takers to combine more than one language skill in the Speaking and Writing sections.
- In the Speaking section, test takers wear headphones and speak into a microphone when they respond. The responses are recorded and transmitted to ETS's Online Scoring Network.
- In the Writing section, test takers must type their responses. Handwriting is not possible.
- Test scores will be reported online. Test takers can see their scores online 4-8 business days after the test and can also receive a copy of their score report by mail.

2 Information on the Reading Section

The Reading section of the TOEFL® iBT measures test takers' ability to understand university-level academic texts. This section has 2 passages, and the length of each passage is about 700 words. Some passages may have underlined words or phrases in blue. Test takers can click on them to see a definition or explanation. Test takers have to answer 10 questions per passage. 35 minutes are given to complete this section, including the time spent reading the passages and answering the questions.

A Types of Reading Passages

- Exposition: Material that provides an explanation of a topic
- Argumentation: Material that presents a point of view about a topic and provides evidence to support it
- Historical narrative: An account of a past event or of a person's life, narrated or written by someone else

B Types of Reading Questions

Type 1 Vocabulary Questions

Vocabulary questions require the test taker to understand specific words or phrases that are used in the passage. These questions ask the test taker to choose another word or phrase that is the most similar in meaning to the highlighted text. The vocabulary words that are highlighted are often important words, so knowing their meanings is often critical for understanding the entire passage. The highlighted words typically have several meanings, so test takers need to be careful to avoid selecting an answer choice simply because it is the word's or phrase's most common meaning.

Type 2 Reference Questions

Reference questions require the test taker to understand the relationship between words and their referents in the passage. These questions most frequently ask the test taker to identify the antecedent of a pronoun. In many cases, the pronouns are words like *he*, *she*, or *they* or *its*, *his*, *hers*, or *theirs*. However, in other cases, relative pronouns like *which* or demonstrative pronouns like *this* or *that* may be asked about instead. This type of question seldom appears on the test anymore.

Type 3 Factual Information Questions

Factual Information questions require the test taker to understand and to be able to recognize facts that are mentioned in the passage. These questions may cover any facts or information that is explicitly covered in the passage. These may appear in the form of details, definitions, explanations, or other kinds of data. The facts which the questions ask about are typically found only in one part of the passage—perhaps in a sentence or two—and do not require a comprehensive understanding of the passage as a whole.

Type 4 Negative Factual Information Questions

Negative Factual Information questions require the test taker to understand and to be able to recognize facts that are mentioned in the passage. These questions may be about any facts or information that is explicitly covered in the passage. However, these questions ask the test taker to identify the incorrect information in the answer choices. Three of the four answer choices will therefore have correct information that can be found in the passage. The answer the test taker must choose will either have incorrect information or information that is not found in the passage.

Type 5 Sentence Simplification Questions

Sentence Simplification questions require the test taker to select a sentence that best restates one that has been highlighted in the passage. These questions ask the test taker to note the main points in the sentence and to make sure that they are mentioned in the rewritten sentence. These sentences use words, phrases, and grammar that are different from the highlighted sentence. They also sometimes do not appear in a passage. When they are asked, there is only one Sentence Simplification question per passage.

Type 6 Inference Questions

Inference questions require the test taker to understand the argument that the passage is attempting to make. These questions ask the test taker to consider the information that is presented and then to come to a logical conclusion about it. The answers to these questions are never explicitly stated in the passage. Instead, the test taker is asked to infer what the author means. These questions often deal with cause and effect or comparisons between two different things, ideas, events, or people.

Type 7 Rhetorical Purpose Questions

Rhetorical Purpose questions require the test taker to understand why the author mentioned or wrote about something in the passage. These questions ask the test taker to consider the reasoning behind the information that is being presented in the passage. For these questions, the function—not the meaning—of the material is the most important aspect to be aware of. The questions often focus on the relationship between the information mentioned or covered either in paragraphs or individual sentences in the passage and the purpose or intention of the information that is given.

Type 8 Insert Text Questions

Insert Text questions require the test taker to determine where in the passage another sentence should be placed. These questions ask the test taker to consider various aspects, including grammar, logic, connecting words, and flow, when deciding where the new sentence best belongs. Recently, there is almost always one Insert Text question per passage. This question always appears just before the last question.

Type 9 Prose Summary Questions

Prose Summary questions require the test taker to understand the main point of the passage and then to select sentences which emphasize the main point. These questions present a sentence which is essentially a thesis statement for the entire passage. The sentence synthesizes the main points of the passage. The test taker must then choose three out of six sentences which most closely describe points mentioned in the introductory sentence. This means that three of the choices are minor points, have incorrect information, or contain information that does not appear in the passage, so they are all therefore incorrect. These are always the last question asked about a Reading passage. Recently, they appear on the test very frequently.

Type 10 Fill in a Table Questions

Fill in a Table questions require the test taker to have a comprehensive understanding of the entire passage. These questions typically break the passage down into two—or sometimes three—main points or themes. The test taker must then read a number of sentences or phrases and determine which of the points or themes the sentences or phrases refer to. These questions often ask the test taker to consider cause and effect, to compare and contrast, or to understand various theories or ideas covered. These are always the last question asked about a Reading passage, but they have become less common recently.

How to Master Skills for the TOEFL® iBT

Actual Test
REDING 2

01

TOEFL READING

Reading Section Directions

This section measures your ability to understand academic passages in English. You will have **35 minutes** to read and answer questions about **2 passages**. A clock at the top of the screen will show you how much time is remaining.

Most questions are worth 1 point but the last question for each passage is worth more than 1 point. The directions for the last question indicate how many points you may receive.

Some passages include a word or phrase that is **underlined** in blue. Click on the word or phrase to see a definition or an explanation.

When you want to move to the next question, click on **Next**. You may skip questions and go back to them later. If you want to return to previous questions, click on **Back**. You can click on **Review** at any time, and the review screen will show you which questions you have answered and which you have not answered. From this review screen, you may go directly to any question you have already seen in the Reading section.

Click on **Continue** to go on.

Causes of the Little Ice Age

The Earth's climate is not static but instead constantly undergoes changes resulting in the planet becoming warmer or cooler than typical. In the past couple of million years, the general condition of the Earth's climate is one of extreme coldness. In fact, the Earth has undergone five major ice ages, the last of which began approximately 2.7 million years ago and is still currently happening. Yet even during this extensive period of time, there have been warm periods interspersed with cool times. For instance, the Medieval Warm Period lasted from roughly 900 to 1300 and was promptly followed by the Little Ice Age, which started around 1300 and did not conclude until around 1850.

Unlike past ice ages, some of which covered virtually the entire planet in thick sheets of ice, the Little Ice Age was a more regional event taking place primarily in the Northern Hemisphere, particularly in Europe and North America. In Europe, **glaciers** rapidly expanded, causing the destruction of mountain villages in the Alps. The River Thames in England froze so solidly that people could ice skate on it in winter. Some places in the Southern Hemisphere, such as New Zealand and Patagonia in South America, also experienced cooler weather. However, other places, such as Africa and eastern China, underwent no period of cooling.

Scientists have long wondered what caused the Little Ice Age and have a number of theories concerning this issue. One factor surely contributing to decreasing temperatures was the lack of sunspot activity on the sun during this period. The Little Ice Age started during the Renaissance and continued into other historical periods, including the Scientific Revolution. It was during these times that men such as Nicholas Copernicus, Galileo Galilei, and Tycho Brahe turned their eyes to the heavens and began making observations. Among those observations were the number of sunspots found on the sun. There were two periods during the Little Ice Age that featured low sunspot activity. They happened from 1450 to 1540 and from 1645 to 1715. Unsurprisingly, these two periods were some of the coolest times of the Little Ice Age.

Sunspots are important to the planet because they are a source of solar radiation, which provides energy capable of reaching the Earth's surface. During periods of high sunspot activity, the Earth receives more solar radiation, and that results in more warmth, which is beneficial both to people and crops. Conversely, when there are fewer sunspots, there is a decline in solar radiation, which frequently causes lower temperatures across the Earth's surface. This is precisely what happened on two different occasions in the middle of the Little Ice Age.

Scientists do not think that lessened sunspot activity was the trigger initiating the Little Ice

Age though. Instead, many scientists believe it was volcanic activity that prompted this period of cooling to begin. Starting in 1257 and continuing until around 1300, there were four violent volcanic eruptions in tropical locations. These volcanoes spewed tremendous amounts of gases and ash into the atmosphere, which resulted in the darkening of the atmosphere and also reflected some of the sun's energy, causing it never to reach the planet. This, in turn, resulted in less sunlight reaching the Earth's surface and therefore made the temperature decline. In addition, there were other large eruptions that happened throughout the Little Ice Age. Among these eruptions was that of Tambora, a volcano in Indonesia, which erupted in 1815 in what is the biggest recorded eruption in history. It was so powerful that the following year was known as the Year Without a Summer.

While the eruptions almost certainly instigated the Little Ice Age, another event that happened afterward is likely the reason it lasted so long. During the 1300s, there was an extended period of time in which Arctic ice melted. Fresh water is not as **dense** as salt water, so the melted ice flowed on top of the ocean and did not mix well with the salt water. Currents bringing warm water from the tropics northward were therefore disrupted, and this caused more cooling to occur and to last for a long time. These three factors together are therefore the likely causes of the Little Ice Age.

Glossary
glacier: a large body of ice that can move forward or backward
dense: thick

Causes of the Little Ice Age

1 → The Earth's climate is not static but instead constantly undergoes changes resulting in the planet becoming warmer or cooler than typical. In the past couple of million years, the general condition of the Earth's climate is one of extreme coldness. In fact, the Earth has undergone five major ice ages, the last of which began approximately 2.7 million years ago and is still currently happening. Yet even during this extensive period of time, there have been warm periods interspersed with cool times. For instance, the Medieval Warm Period lasted from roughly 900 to 1300 and was promptly followed by the Little Ice Age, which started around 1300 and did not conclude until around 1850.

1. The word "static" in the passage is closest in meaning to
   - Ⓐ variable
   - Ⓑ unique
   - Ⓒ fixed
   - Ⓓ violent

2. In paragraph 1, the author uses "the Medieval Warm Period" as an example of
   - Ⓐ a time when the Earth's climate changed from warm to cold
   - Ⓑ the hottest period of time in the past few centuries
   - Ⓒ a time when many glaciers on the planet disappeared
   - Ⓓ a period when civilization thrived thanks to the warm weather

2 → Unlike past ice ages, some of which covered virtually the entire planet in thick sheets of ice, the Little Ice Age was a more regional event taking place primarily in the Northern Hemisphere, particularly in Europe and North America. In Europe, **glaciers** rapidly expanded, causing the destruction of mountain villages in the Alps. The River Thames in England froze so solidly that people could ice skate on it in winter. Some places in the Southern Hemisphere, such as New Zealand and Patagonia in South America, also experienced cooler weather. However, other places, such as Africa and eastern China, underwent no period of cooling.

3. According to paragraph 2, which of the following is true of the Little Ice Age?
   - Ⓐ It cooled the climate in most places around the world.
   - Ⓑ It had very powerful effects in places in Europe.
   - Ⓒ It made places in Africa much colder than normal.
   - Ⓓ It resulted in places like Patagonia getting warm weather.

Glossary

glacier: a large body of ice that can move forward or backward

³ → Scientists have long wondered what caused the Little Ice Age and have a number of theories concerning this issue. One factor surely contributing to decreasing temperatures was the lack of sunspot activity on the sun during this period. The Little Ice Age started during the Renaissance and continued into other historical periods, including the Scientific Revolution. It was during these times that men such as Nicholas Copernicus, Galileo Galilei, and Tycho Brahe turned their eyes to the heavens and began making observations. Among those observations were the number of sunspots found on the sun. There were two periods during the Little Ice Age that featured low sunspot activity. They happened from 1450 to 1540 and from 1645 to 1715. Unsurprisingly, these two periods were some of the coolest times of the Little Ice Age.

4. In paragraph 3, the author implies that sunspots

   Ⓐ tend to disappear for just a few years at a time
   Ⓑ can easily be predicted by astronomers watching the sun
   Ⓒ can have a direct effect on how hot or cold the Earth is
   Ⓓ often send large amounts of energy out into space

⁴→ Sunspots are important to the planet because they are a source of solar radiation, which provides energy capable of reaching the Earth's surface. During periods of high sunspot activity, the Earth receives more solar radiation, and that results in more warmth, which is beneficial both to people and crops. Conversely, when there are fewer sunspots, there is a decline in solar radiation, which frequently causes lower temperatures across the Earth's surface. This is precisely what happened on two different occasions in the middle of the Little Ice Age.

5. In paragraph 4, all of the following questions are answered EXCEPT:
    A. How does solar radiation cause harm to the planet?
    B. In what way can sunspots affect the Earth's climate?
    C. How many times were there few sunspots during the Little Ice Age?
    D. What makes sunspots important to the Earth?

⁵→ Scientists do not think that lessened sunspot activity was the trigger initiating the Little Ice Age though. Instead, many scientists believe it was volcanic activity that prompted this period of cooling to begin. Starting in 1257 and continuing until around 1300, there were four violent volcanic eruptions in tropical locations. These volcanoes spewed tremendous amounts of gases and ash into the atmosphere, which resulted in the darkening of the atmosphere and also reflected some of the sun's energy, causing it never to reach the planet. This, in turn, resulted in less sunlight reaching the Earth's surface and therefore made the temperature decline. In addition, there were other large eruptions that happened throughout the Little Ice Age. Among these eruptions was that of Tambora, a volcano in Indonesia, which erupted in 1815 in what is the biggest recorded eruption in history. It was so powerful that the following year was known as the Year Without a Summer.

6. According to paragraph 5, the Little Ice Age probably started because

Ⓐ the sun had few or no sunspots for a period lasting decades
Ⓑ the volcano Tambora erupted in the most powerful recorded eruption ever
Ⓒ a combination of factors, including natural phenomena, took place
Ⓓ volcanic eruptions prevented the sun's light from reaching the Earth

7. Which of the following can be inferred from paragraph 5 about the Year Without a Summer?

Ⓐ The average global temperature was the lowest on record.
Ⓑ It was one of the coldest years of the Little Ice Age.
Ⓒ Millions of people died of starvation during that time.
Ⓓ It was caused by multiple volcanic eruptions.

While the eruptions almost certainly instigated the Little Ice Age, another event that happened afterward is likely the reason it lasted so long. During the 1300s, there was an extended period of time in which Arctic ice melted. Fresh water is not as **dense** as salt water, so the melted ice flowed on top of the ocean and did not mix well with the salt water. Currents bringing warm water from the tropics northward were therefore disrupted, and this caused more cooling to occur and to last for a long time. These three factors together are therefore the likely causes of the Little Ice Age.

8. Which of the sentences below best expresses the essential information in the highlighted sentence in the passage? *Incorrect* answer choices change the meaning in important ways or leave out essential information.

    A) Warm weather from the tropics was unable to move north, so the weather became colder than before.
    B) It was not possible for any warm water to go to the north, so people in those areas suffered cold weather.
    C) The weather got colder for a long time because of disruptions to currents bringing warm water north.
    D) The tropics were warm during this time, but then they became much cooler for a long amount of time.

Glossary
dense: thick

Scientists do not think that lessened sunspot activity was the trigger initiating the Little Ice Age though. Instead, many scientists believe it was volcanic activity that prompted this period of cooling to begin. Starting in 1257 and continuing until around 1300, there were four violent volcanic eruptions in tropical locations. **[1]** These volcanoes spewed tremendous amounts of gases and ash into the atmosphere, which resulted in the darkening of the atmosphere and also reflected some of the sun's energy, causing it never to reach the planet. **[2]** This, in turn, resulted in less sunlight reaching the Earth's surface and therefore made the temperature decline. **[3]** In addition, there were other large eruptions that happened throughout the Little Ice Age. **[4]** Among these eruptions was that of Tambora, a volcano in Indonesia, which erupted in 1815 in what is the biggest recorded eruption in history. It was so powerful that the following year was known as the Year Without a Summer.

9. Look at the four squares [■] that indicate where the following sentence could be added to the passage.

   One of them, at Mount Samalas in Indonesia, was one of the most powerful eruptions in millions of years.

   Where would the sentence best fit?

   Click on a square [■] to add the sentence to the passage.

10 Directions: An introductory sentence for a brief summary of the passage is provided below. Complete the summary by selecting the THREE answer choices that express the most important ideas of the passage. Some sentences do not belong because they express ideas that are not presented in the passage or are minor ideas in the passage. **This question is worth 2 points.**

Drag your answer choices to the spaces where they belong.
To remove an answer choice, click on it. To review the passage, click on **View Text**.

Scientists have some theories on what caused the Little Ice Age.

-
-
-

Answer Choices

1. The Medieval Warm Period happened right before the Little Ice Age did.

2. When there were few sunspots, the weather during that time period became colder.

3. The volcano Tambora was the most powerful eruption people ever witnessed.

4. Melting ice from the Arctic cooled the weather for a long period of time.

5. Less solar radiation than normal reaches the Earth when there are more sunspots.

6. Powerful volcanic eruptions are probably what made the Little Ice Age begin.

Polar Exploration

A statue of Roald Amundsen

The North and South poles were among the last places on the Earth reached by humans in the great age of exploration at the end of the nineteenth century and the beginning of the twentieth century. The story of their exploration is a tale of ambition, fraud, and great heroics with men eager to be hailed as the conquerors of the poles forced to the limits of human endurance. The main players on this stage were Americans Frederick Cook and Robert Peary, Norwegian Roald Amundsen, and the tragic Robert Scott of Britain. While Cook and Peary took part in expeditions to both regions, they are best known for the controversy surrounding their claim of reaching the North Pole. Both poles had heroes and villains, and both have differences and similarities.

The North and South poles are at the geographic **terminus** of the Earth's axis, both represented by ninety degrees latitude north and south. While the South Pole sits atop a 3,000-meter ice sheet covering the landmass of Antarctica, the North Pole stands atop a constantly shifting and cracking field of ice covering the Arctic Ocean. Navigation at both poles is difficult, and explorers need to make precise calculations to ensure they are actually at the pole. In the early twentieth century, navigation practices were still in the dark ages compared to today. Navigation and its problems were at the core of the controversy, which persists to this day, over who reached the North Pole first.

Frederick Cook claimed to have reached the North Pole on April 21, 1908, with two Inuit men after a trip over the ice from Greenland. He announced his claim almost one year later when his team barely survived the return trip. At the same time, on April 6, 1909, Robert Peary and five other men, four of whom were Inuit, also claimed to have reached the North Pole. Cook's claim was not backed up by accurate navigation records, which he said were lost. His two companions stated they had never left sight of land and had wandered for weeks, seemingly lost, meaning Cook deliberately committed fraud. Robert Peary's claim is much stronger but is also questionable since nobody else in his party could navigate and their journey from their last camp to the pole was made at an amazing pace compared to other similar journeys. Most experts now agree that Peary thought he had reached the North Pole but was perhaps five miles from it.

However, there is no doubt who reached the South Pole first. In 1911, a Norwegian expedition led by Amundsen and a British expedition led by Scott set out for the South Pole. While both teams spent time building advance supply points, Amundsen's team had the advantage of choosing a base camp sixty miles closer than the British. His group also used dog sled teams and skis while the British used horses and brute manpower to move supplies and were reluctant to learn to use skis. Ultimately, Amundsen's team reached the pole first on December 14, 1911, with Scott's team arriving a month later to find a note penned by Amundsen. Amundsen's team safely returned to its base camp, but Scott's team, weakened by injuries and illness, stalled eleven miles from a supply point and could not continue. By the end of March 1912, they were all dead. It was later asserted that faulty navigation had placed the supply point thirty miles north of where it should have been.

Scott became a tragic figure of the age of exploration, and his story overshadowed the Norwegian team's accomplishment. Amundsen himself died in the Arctic region, leading a flight searching for some lost explorers in 1928. Peary went on to international acclaim for his achievements, but a shadow of doubt has always been associated with his North Pole exploration, and Cook's name will forever be affixed to his fraudulent claims. One only needs to point to navigation as the key to both explorations, and in this regard, Amundsen was the master of the others. He took great pains to make sure his progress was accurate and recorded everything. Undoubtedly, he had learned from the mistakes of Peary and Cook and knew his claim had to be airtight to be accepted.

Glossary
terminus: the end of something

Polar Exploration

¹ ➛ The North and South poles were among the last places on the Earth reached by humans in the great age of exploration at the end of the nineteenth century and the beginning of the twentieth century. The story of their exploration is a tale of ambition, fraud, and great heroics with men eager to be hailed as the conquerors of the poles forced to the limits of human endurance. The main players on this stage were Americans Frederick Cook and Robert Peary, Norwegian Roald Amundsen, and the tragic Robert Scott of Britain. While Cook and Peary took part in expeditions to both regions, they are best known for the controversy surrounding their claim of reaching the North Pole. Both poles had heroes and villains, and both have differences and similarities.

11 According to paragraph 1, one of the main reasons men tried to reach the two poles was to

Ⓐ claim them as territory for their countries

Ⓑ find out the best ways to navigate in those areas

Ⓒ become world renowned as great explorers

Ⓓ test their power to tolerate difficulties in a contest

2 → The North and South poles are at the geographic **terminus** of the Earth's axis, both represented by ninety degrees latitude north and south. While the South Pole sits atop a 3,000-meter ice sheet covering the landmass of Antarctica, the North Pole stands atop a constantly shifting and cracking field of ice covering the Arctic Ocean. Navigation at both poles is difficult, and explorers need to make precise calculations to ensure they are actually at the pole. In the early twentieth century, navigation practices were still in the dark ages compared to today. Navigation and its problems were at the core of the controversy, which persists to this day, over who reached the North Pole first.

12 The word "core" in the passage is closest in meaning to
- A center
- B sample
- C essence
- D staple

13 According to paragraph 2, all of the following are characteristic of the two poles EXCEPT:
- A Both are covered in sheets of ice.
- B Both are difficult to navigate to.
- C Both are at 90 degrees latitude.
- D Both are sitting on a landmass.

Glossary
terminus: the end of something

3 → Frederick Cook claimed to have reached the North Pole on April 21, 1908, with two Inuit men after a trip over the ice from Greenland. He announced his claim almost one year later when his team barely survived the return trip. At the same time, on April 6, 1909, Robert Peary and five other men, four of whom were Inuit, also claimed to have reached the North Pole. Cook's claim was not backed up by accurate navigation records, which he said were lost. His two companions stated they had never left sight of land and had wandered for weeks, seemingly lost, meaning Cook deliberately committed fraud. Robert Peary's claim is much stronger but is also questionable since nobody else in his party could navigate and their journey from their last camp to the pole was made at an amazing pace compared to other similar journeys. Most experts now agree that Peary thought he had reached the North Pole but was perhaps five miles from it.

14 According to paragraph 3, why is Frederick Cook's claim to have been the first to reach the North Pole in question?
Click on 2 answers.

Ⓐ His records of his navigation calculations were lost.

Ⓑ His team members did not agree with his assertions.

Ⓒ His team's speed was unprecedented for the Arctic.

Ⓓ He was not qualified as a navigator in the Arctic.

However, there is no doubt who reached the South Pole first. In 1911, a Norwegian expedition led by Amundsen and a British expedition led by Scott set out for the South Pole. While both teams spent time building advance supply points, Amundsen's team had the advantage of choosing a base camp sixty miles closer than the British. His group also used dog sled teams and skis while the British used horses and brute manpower to move supplies and were reluctant to learn to use skis. Ultimately, Amundsen's team reached the pole first on December 14, 1911, with Scott's team arriving a month later to find a note penned by Amundsen. ==Amundsen's team safely returned to its base camp, but Scott's team, weakened by injuries and illness, stalled eleven miles from a supply point and could not continue.== By the end of March 1912, they were all dead. It was later asserted that faulty navigation had placed the supply point thirty miles north of where it should have been.

15 Which of the sentences below best expresses the essential information in the highlighted sentence in the passage? *Incorrect* answer choices change the meaning in important ways or leave out essential information.

(A) While Amundsen's team got back to its base camp, Scott's team could not move forward because it failed to find a supply point.

(B) Scott's team was too weak to find its supplies and continue its expedition while Amundsen's team made it back to its base camp.

(C) While Amundsen's team returned safely, Scott's team became weak and failed because the supplies it needed were in the wrong place.

(D) Amundsen's base camp was closer than Scott's supplies, so Amundsen's team returned safely while Scott's did not.

4 → However, there is no doubt who reached the South Pole first. In 1911, a Norwegian expedition led by Amundsen and a British expedition led by Scott set out for the South Pole. While both teams spent time building advance supply points, Amundsen's team had the advantage of choosing a base camp sixty miles closer than the British. His group also used dog sled teams and skis while the British used horses and brute manpower to move supplies and were reluctant to learn to use skis. Ultimately, Amundsen's team reached the pole first on December 14, 1911, with Scott's team arriving a month later to find a note penned by Amundsen. Amundsen's team safely returned to its base camp, but Scott's team, weakened by injuries and illness, stalled eleven miles from a supply point and could not continue. By the end of March 1912, they were all dead. It was later asserted that faulty navigation had placed the supply point thirty miles north of where it should have been.

16 In paragraph 4, the author mentions the advantages that the Norwegians had over the British in order to

Ⓐ prove that the British were not familiar with Antarctic exploration

Ⓑ show why the Norwegians were the first to reach the South Pole

Ⓒ claim that the British would have been first if they had been more prepared

Ⓓ propose that the Norwegians had an unfair advantage over the British

17 In paragraph 4, the author implies that Robert Scott's team

Ⓐ departed for the South Pole at the wrong time of the year

Ⓑ was found by Amundsen's team after they got lost

Ⓒ suffered from illness on the way to the South Pole

Ⓓ could have survived by placing the supply point properly

5 → Scott became a tragic figure of the age of exploration, and his story overshadowed the Norwegian team's accomplishment. Amundsen himself died in the Arctic region, leading a flight searching for some lost explorers in 1928. Peary went on to international acclaim for his achievements, but a shadow of doubt has always been associated with his North Pole exploration, and Cook's name will forever be affixed to his fraudulent claims. One only needs to point to navigation as the key to both explorations, and in this regard, Amundsen was the master of the others. He took great pains to make sure his progress was accurate and recorded everything. Undoubtedly, he had learned from the mistakes of Peary and Cook and knew his claim had to be airtight to be accepted.

18 It can be inferred from paragraph 5 that Amundsen's claims to have reached the South Pole first were confirmed by

Ⓐ his navigation records
Ⓑ his team members
Ⓒ Scott's team
Ⓓ Cook and Peary

Frederick Cook claimed to have reached the North Pole on April 21, 1908, with two Inuit men after a trip over the ice from Greenland. He announced his claim almost one year later when his team barely survived the return trip. ■ At the same time, on April 6, 1909, Robert Peary and five other men, four of whom were Inuit, also claimed to have reached the North Pole. ■ Cook's claim was not backed up by accurate navigation records, which he said were lost. ■ His two companions stated they had never left sight of land and had wandered for weeks, seemingly lost, meaning Cook deliberately committed fraud. ■ Robert Peary's claim is much stronger but is also questionable since nobody else in his party could navigate and their journey from their last camp to the pole was made at an amazing pace compared to other similar journeys. Most experts now agree that Peary thought he had reached the North Pole but was perhaps five miles from it.

19 Look at the four squares [■] that indicate where the following sentence could be added to the passage.

Cook was also involved in an earlier controversy over his claims, later proved false, that he had been the first to climb Mount McKinley in Alaska, the highest mountain in the United States.

Where would the sentence best fit?

Click on a square [■] to add the sentence to the passage.

20 Directions: An introductory sentence for a brief summary of the passage is provided below. Complete the summary by selecting the THREE answer choices that express the most important ideas of the passage. Some sentences do not belong because they express ideas that are not presented in the passage or are minor ideas in the passage. **This question is worth 2 points.**

Drag your answer choices to the spaces where they belong.
To remove an answer choice, click on it. To review the passage, click on **View Text**.

Several teams were involved in the races to be the first to reach the North and South poles.

-
-
-

Answer Choices

1. Experts agree that Robert Peary was correct in stating he was the first to the North Pole.
2. Roald Amundsen and his team made it to the South Pole first in 1911.
3. Many of the first teams that tried to get to the two poles were involved in controversies.
4. Bringing the proper equipment was vital to the survival of teams at the poles.
5. There is a dispute as to whether Frederick Cook and Robert Peary ever made it to the North Pole.
6. Robert Scott's team was not prepared for the journey, so they all died.

How to
Master Skills for the
TOEFL® iBT

Actual
Test
READING 2

02

TOEFL READING

Reading Section Directions

This section measures your ability to understand academic passages in English. You will have **35 minutes** to read and answer questions about **2 passages**. A clock at the top of the screen will show you how much time is remaining.

Most questions are worth 1 point but the last question for each passage is worth more than 1 point. The directions for the last question indicate how many points you may receive.

Some passages include a word or phrase that is **underlined** in blue. Click on the word or phrase to see a definition or an explanation.

When you want to move to the next question, click on **Next**. You may skip questions and go back to them later. If you want to return to previous questions, click on **Back**. You can click on **Review** at any time, and the review screen will show you which questions you have answered and which you have not answered. From this review screen, you may go directly to any question you have already seen in the Reading section.

Click on **Continue** to go on.

The Formation of the Inner and Outer Planets

The planets of the solar system

Most astronomers agree that the sun formed approximately 4.6 billion years ago. Not long afterward, the eight planets in the solar system—Mercury, Venus, Earth, Mars, Jupiter, Saturn, Uranus, and Neptune—began to undergo the extensive process of formation. How the planets formed is something that humans who looked up at the night sky have wondered about for centuries. Thanks to modern technology, particularly telescopes, astronomers have come up with the Nebular Hypothesis, which provides an explanation for how the planets were formed and is now accepted by the majority of astronomers.

According to the Nebular Hypothesis, the sun formed from a nebula, which is a gigantic cloud of gas and dust. Something such as a passing star or a **supernova** caused a gravitational collapse to occur in the middle of the cloud, which subsequently resulted in dust and gas pockets collecting in various places. These pockets started rotating, and most of the material moved to the center, which led to the creation of the sun. Other material, however, remained outside the center, formed something called a **protoplanetary disk**, and would proceed to create the planets.

One important fact to remember is that the protoplanetary disk had temperatures that varied from place to place. The closer the material in the disk was to the sun, the hotter it was. Rocky and metallic materials condense at higher temperatures, so they tended to be closer to the sun. On the other hand, water, methane, and other hydrogen compounds condense at lower temperatures, so they were typically farther from the sun. In addition, there was something called the frost line, which is the dividing line for different types of planets in the solar system. The frost line was where variances in temperature caused the creation of two types of planets.

The four planets that are the closest to the sun are called the terrestrial planets. These planets are formed primarily of rocky material. These rocks, which were mostly formed with heavy elements and minerals, orbited the sun at roughly the same speed. When they collided with one another, they usually stuck together instead of causing destruction. Over time, due to the process of accretion, the pieces became larger, and then gravity made them assume spherical shapes. Since there was a relatively limited amount of metallic and rocky material in the nebula, the sizes of Mercury, Venus, Earth, and Mars are fairly small.

The four other planets—Jupiter, Saturn, Uranus, and Neptune—formed beyond the frost line, so they contained a much smaller content of rocky and metallic material. Instead, due to cooler temperatures, the hydrogen compounds in the protoplanetary disk condensed into various ices. As more of this type of material came together, the four new planets became larger and larger. Their gravity became more powerful, which enabled them to pull in even more material, particularly hydrogen and helium in their gaseous forms. This caused the planets, especially Jupiter and Saturn, to become enormous in size. The Jovian planets, as the four outer planets are frequently called, developed dense icy cores that were surrounded by large amounts of gas. At some point, they likely grew so large that they caused gravitational collapses, so some of the rocky material in them wound up forming the dozens of moons that orbit these planets.

The Nebular Hypothesis also accounts for other objects in the solar system, such as the Asteroid Belt and the numerous dwarf planets that orbit the sun in the Kuiper Belt and the Oort Cloud. It attributes the countless asteroids in the Asteroid Belt to a fifth rocky planet that was ripped apart by the strength of Jupiter's gravity. In addition, leftover debris that never formed any of the eight planets wound up creating the dwarf planets. While this process appears simple, it required a long amount of time to occur. Jupiter and Saturn likely formed relatively rapidly in approximately ten million years whereas Uranus and Neptune may have required up to ninety million years to form. As for the terrestrial planets, astronomers believe they took at least 100 million years to form while some even claim the process might have required at least 400 million years.

Glossary
supernova: the extremely powerful explosion of a star
protoplanetary disk: a spinning mass of gas and dust that eventually forms a planet

The Formation of the Inner and Outer Planets

1 → Most astronomers agree that the sun formed approximately 4.6 billion years ago. Not long afterward, the eight planets in the solar system—Mercury, Venus, Earth, Mars, Jupiter, Saturn, Uranus, and Neptune—began to undergo the extensive process of formation. How the planets formed is something that humans who looked up at the night sky have wondered about for centuries. Thanks to modern technology, particularly telescopes, astronomers have come up with the Nebular Hypothesis, which provides an explanation for how the planets were formed and is now accepted by the majority of astronomers.

1 In paragraph 1, why does the author mention "telescopes"?

Ⓐ To credit them for being able to observe the planets closely

Ⓑ To claim they resulted in the creation of the Nebular Hypothesis

Ⓒ To discuss the two main types of telescopes used by astronomers

Ⓓ To compare their usage in the present with their usage in the past

2 → According to the Nebular Hypothesis, the sun formed from a nebula, which is a gigantic cloud of gas and dust. Something such as a passing star or a **supernova** caused a gravitational collapse to occur in the middle of the cloud, which subsequently resulted in dust and gas pockets collecting in various places. These pockets started rotating, and most of the material moved to the center, which led to the creation of the sun. Other material, however, remained outside the center, formed something called a **protoplanetary disk**, and would proceed to create the planets.

2. In paragraph 2, all of the following questions are answered EXCEPT:
   A) How large was the nebula that formed Earth's solar system?
   B) What might have been the reason a gravitational collapse happened?
   C) What does the Nebular Hypothesis state about the sun's formation?
   D) What are the primary components of a nebula?

Glossary

supernova: the extremely powerful explosion of a star
protoplanetary disk: a spinning mass of gas and dust that eventually forms a planet

³ ➡ One important fact to remember is that the protoplanetary disk had temperatures that varied from place to place. The closer the material in the disk was to the sun, the hotter it was. Rocky and metallic materials condense at higher temperatures, so they tended to be closer to the sun. On the other hand, water, methane, and other hydrogen compounds condense at lower temperatures, so they were typically farther from the sun. In addition, there was something called the frost line, which is the dividing line for different types of planets in the solar system. The frost line was where variances in temperature caused the creation of two types of planets.

3 The word "variances" in the passage is closest in meaning to
  Ⓐ regulations
  Ⓑ differences
  Ⓒ moderations
  Ⓓ increases

4 In paragraph 3, the author implies that the planets close to the sun
  Ⓐ are all very similar in size to one another
  Ⓑ took longer to form than the planets far from the sun
  Ⓒ are all located beyond the frost line
  Ⓓ are comprised largely of rocky material and metal

5 According to paragraph 3, which of the following is true of the frost line?
  Ⓐ It is close to stars that are fairly small in size.
  Ⓑ Most solar systems have planets located inside them.
  Ⓒ Planets on either side of it are different in composition.
  Ⓓ Astronomers were able to determine its location easily.

The four planets that are the closest to the sun are called the terrestrial planets. These planets are formed primarily of rocky material. These rocks, which were mostly formed with heavy elements and minerals, orbited the sun at roughly the same speed. When they collided with one another, they usually stuck together instead of causing destruction. Over time, due to the process of accretion, the pieces became larger, and then gravity made them assume spherical shapes. Since there was a relatively limited amount of metallic and rocky material in the nebula, the sizes of Mercury, Venus, Earth, and Mars are fairly small.

6. Which of the sentences below best expresses the essential information in the highlighted sentence in the passage? *Incorrect* answer choices change the meaning in important ways or leave out essential information.

   Ⓐ Four of the planets that orbit the sun were created with metallic and rocky material.

   Ⓑ The lack of certain materials in the nebula made some planets become small in size.

   Ⓒ The nebula had a limited amount of some materials, which went into four planets.

   Ⓓ The first four planets that orbit the sun are comprised of metal and rocky material.

⁵ ➡ The four other planets—Jupiter, Saturn, Uranus, and Neptune—formed beyond the frost line, so they contained a much smaller content of rocky and metallic material. Instead, due to cooler temperatures, the hydrogen compounds in the protoplanetary disk condensed into various ices. As more of this type of material came together, the four new planets became larger and larger. Their gravity became more powerful, which enabled them to pull in even more material, particularly hydrogen and helium in their gaseous forms. This caused the planets, especially Jupiter and Saturn, to become enormous in size. The Jovian planets, as the four outer planets are frequently called, developed dense icy cores that were surrounded by large amounts of gas. At some point, they likely grew so large that they caused gravitational collapses, so some of the rocky material in them wound up forming the dozens of moons that orbit these planets.

7 Select the TWO answer choices from paragraph 5 that identify how the Jovian planets formed. *To receive credit, you must select TWO answers.*

Ⓐ They were created with large amounts of hydrogen ices.
Ⓑ They developed dense cores formed with heavy metals.
Ⓒ They attracted more rocky material than the terrestrial planets.
Ⓓ Their gravity helped them attract certain types of gases.

⁶ ➜ The Nebular Hypothesis also accounts for other objects in the solar system, such as the Asteroid Belt and the numerous dwarf planets that orbit the sun in the Kuiper Belt and the Oort Cloud. It attributes the countless asteroids in the Asteroid Belt to a fifth rocky planet that was ripped apart by the strength of Jupiter's gravity. In addition, leftover debris that never formed any of the eight planets wound up creating the dwarf planets. While this process appears simple, it required a long amount of time to occur. Jupiter and Saturn likely formed relatively rapidly in approximately ten million years whereas Uranus and Neptune may have required up to ninety million years to form. As for the terrestrial planets, astronomers believe they took at least 100 million years to form while some even claim the process might have required at least 400 million years.

8. The author discusses "the Asteroid Belt" in paragraph 6 in order to

   Ⓐ mention its location in the solar system
   Ⓑ point out some of the large asteroids in it
   Ⓒ focus on how it was most likely created
   Ⓓ compare it with the Kuiper Belt

The four other planets—Jupiter, Saturn, Uranus, and Neptune—formed beyond the frost line, so they contained a much smaller content of rocky and metallic material. Instead, due to cooler temperatures, the hydrogen compounds in the protoplanetary disk condensed into various ices. As more of this type of material came together, the four new planets became larger and larger. Their gravity became more powerful, which enabled them to pull in even more material, particularly hydrogen and helium in their gaseous forms. ■ This caused the planets, especially Jupiter and Saturn, to become enormous in size. ■ The Jovian planets, as the four outer planets are frequently called, developed dense icy cores that were surrounded by large amounts of gas. ■ At some point, they likely grew so large that they caused gravitational collapses, so some of the rocky material in them wound up forming the dozens of moons that orbit these planets. ■

9. Look at the four squares [■] that indicate where the following sentence could be added to the passage.

   As of 2023, Neptune has the fewest at sixteen while Saturn has 146 of them.

   Where would the sentence best fit?

   Click on a square [■] to add the sentence to the passage.

Directions: An introductory sentence for a brief summary of the passage is provided below. Complete the summary by selecting the THREE answer choices that express the most important ideas of the passage. Some sentences do not belong because they express ideas that are not presented in the passage or are minor ideas in the passage. **This question is worth 2 points.**

Drag your answer choices to the spaces where they belong.
To remove an answer choice, click on it. To review the passage, click on **View Text**.

The Nebular Hypothesis explains how the planets orbiting the sun were probably formed.

-
-
-

Answer Choices

1. Ices that were created at low temperatures led to the forming of the Jovian planets.

2. The invention of the telescope let astronomers come up with the Nebular Hypothesis.

3. The frost line explains why planets close to the sun can be somewhat large in size.

4. Some material from the nebula led to the creation of dwarf planets in the Oort Cloud.

5. The terrestrial planets formed from rock and metal and are close to the sun.

6. The material that created everything in the solar system came from a large nebula.

Agriculture and Urbanization

In the modern world, many people take the **procurement** of food for granted, especially in industrialized states. Even in many countries with marginalized economies, there is enough food for all. It is just unevenly distributed with a powerful elite living lives of luxury in lands rife with deprivation and starvation. An abundance of food is not the norm of human history. For the first tens of thousands of years, humans lived literal hand-to-mouth existences as hunter-gatherers, waking each morning with one thought in mind: how to find something to eat. The fruits and roots of the plants they gathered and the flesh of the fish they caught and the animals they hunted were their sole sources of nourishment. This overwhelming need occupied most of their time and left them with little to improve their lives in other ways. Permanent settlements were unheard of as each band or tribe moved from place to place in search of new sources of food. It was not until man learned the mysteries of agriculture about 12,000 years ago that man had a renewable source of nourishment and formed the first permanent settlements.

All of the main staple crops in the world at one time grew in the wild, often in different forms than are used today. The cultivation of these plants in regularly planted fields constitutes the beginnings of agriculture, and coupled with the domestication of animals, it marked the first real civilizations on the Earth. Prior to this point, in approximately 10,000 B.C., there was nothing to unify humans in any large groupings. In fact, large groupings would have been detrimental to the survival of the group as the food from their natural surroundings could only support a limited number of people. How and why man first began the process of planting crops, harvesting them, and storing them for future use is still not entirely understood. Nevertheless, there are five undisputed original centers of agriculture: the eastern United States, the area of southern Mexico and Guatemala, the Andes Mountain region of modern Peru, the Fertile Crescent region in the modern Middle East, and eastern China.

All five independently developed agriculture from the plant species available in their regions. With the exception of the eastern United States, in ancient times, all became centers of urbanization with the Fertile Crescent area the most likely site of man's first towns and cities. Agriculture is a labor-intensive activity requiring a large group of people to live in the same place for continuous periods. Once an area was cleared of trees, stones, or other obstacles and crops were planted, it made sense to remain there and to settle permanently. The crops also needed to be protected from animals and those still leading nomadic lives. Undoubtedly, agriculture gave rise to urbanization and not the reverse since without agriculture there was no reason to establish permanent settlements.

With a surplus of food available, people had time to take part in activities other than food procurement. Artisans, merchants, scholars, engineers, priests, bureaucrats, permanent garrisons, and a myriad of others were fed by the surplus labor of the masses. For the first time in human history, a distinction grew between different groups of people: those who grew the food and those who did not. Perversely, those who did not grow the food became more powerful by using their free time to plan cities and temples, develop weapons, gather armies, and wage war on their fellow humans. The masses of people became tied to the land and labored for the few elites at the top.

A distinction also grew between those who lived in cities and enjoyed their vices and those who remained on farms. In the ancient world, cities became places of danger where crime was rife, illness spread, and the worst sins of mankind were perpetrated, a situation that remains unchanged today. Much of humanity now resides in cities despite modern urban ills. Most of mankind has been free of its daily search for sustenance, thereby allowing humans to progress a tremendous deal farther in 12,000 years than in all man's previous history. Yet this progress has been with much pain with the rise of powerful elites and a world of haves and have-nots.

Glossary
procurement: the process of obtaining a supply of something

Agriculture and Urbanization

1 → In the modern world, many people take the **procurement** of food for granted, especially in industrialized states. Even in many countries with marginalized economies, there is enough food for all. It is just unevenly distributed with a powerful elite living lives of luxury in lands rife with deprivation and starvation. An abundance of food is not the norm of human history. For the first tens of thousands of years, humans lived literal hand-to-mouth existences as hunter-gatherers, waking each morning with one thought in mind: how to find something to eat. The fruits and roots of the plants they gathered and the flesh of the fish they caught and the animals they hunted were their sole sources of nourishment. This overwhelming need occupied most of their time and left them with little to improve their lives in other ways. Permanent settlements were unheard of as each band or tribe moved from place to place in search of new sources of food. It was not until man learned the mysteries of agriculture about 12,000 years ago that man had a renewable source of nourishment and formed the first permanent settlements.

Glossary

procurement: the process of obtaining a supply of something

---

11 The word "deprivation" in the passage is closest in meaning to
 Ⓐ privacy
 Ⓑ distress
 Ⓒ desire
 Ⓓ poverty

12 According to paragraph 1, in many countries with marginalized economies
 Ⓐ there is enough food only for a select elite
 Ⓑ food is not shared fairly by everyone
 Ⓒ everyone gets more than enough food
 Ⓓ select elites decide who gets the food

2 → All of the main staple crops in the world at one time grew in the wild, often in different forms than are used today. The cultivation of these plants in regularly planted fields constitutes the beginnings of agriculture, and coupled with the domestication of animals, it marked the first real civilizations on the Earth. Prior to this point, in approximately 10,000 B.C., there was nothing to unify humans in any large groupings. In fact, large groupings would have been detrimental to the survival of the group as the food from their natural surroundings could only support a limited number of people. How and why man first began the process of planting crops, harvesting them, and storing them for future use is still not entirely understood. Nevertheless, there are five undisputed original centers of agriculture: the eastern United States, the area of southern Mexico and Guatemala, the Andes Mountain region of modern Peru, the Fertile Crescent region in the modern Middle East, and eastern China.

13 Which of the sentences below best expresses the essential information in the highlighted sentence in the passage? *Incorrect* answer choices change the meaning in important ways or leave out essential information.

- A Large groups could not exist because there was not enough food in a given area for everyone to live on.
- B Large groups were needed to survive because they could gather more food from a given area.
- C The size of a group depended on the amount of food in a given area and its natural surroundings.
- D Survival was dependent on the size of the group and the amount of food its members could bring with them.

14 In paragraph 2, the author's description of early agriculture mentions all of the following EXCEPT:

- A Where humans first began to grow crops
- B How humans first managed to grow crops
- C When humans developed the first crops
- D The origins of the crops that are common today

3 → All five independently developed agriculture from the plant species available in their regions. With the exception of the eastern United States, in ancient times, all became centers of urbanization with the Fertile Crescent area the most likely site of man's first towns and cities. Agriculture is a labor-intensive activity requiring a large group of people to live in the same place for continuous periods. Once an area was cleared of trees, stones, or other obstacles and crops were planted, it made sense to remain there and to settle permanently. The crops also needed to be protected from animals and those still leading nomadic lives. Undoubtedly, agriculture gave rise to urbanization and not the reverse since without agriculture there was no reason to establish permanent settlements.

15 According to paragraph 3, each original area of agriculture

Ⓐ had the same plants from wild sources
Ⓑ shared plants between different areas
Ⓒ used the plants found in its own area
Ⓓ had some plants that were in common

4 ➜ With a surplus of food available, people had time to take part in activities other than food procurement. Artisans, merchants, scholars, engineers, priests, bureaucrats, permanent garrisons, and a myriad of others were fed by the surplus labor of the masses. For the first time in human history, a distinction grew between different groups of people: those who grew the food and those who did not. Perversely, those who did not grow the food became more powerful by using their free time to plan cities and temples, develop weapons, gather armies, and wage war on their fellow humans. The masses of people became tied to the land and labored for the few elites at the top.

5 ➜ A distinction also grew between those who lived in cities and enjoyed their vices and those who remained on farms. In the ancient world, cities became places of danger where crime was rife, illness spread, and the worst sins of mankind were perpetrated, a situation that remains unchanged today. Much of humanity now resides in cities despite modern urban ills. Most of mankind has been free of its daily search for sustenance, thereby allowing humans to progress a tremendous deal farther in 12,000 years than in all man's previous history. Yet this progress has been with much pain with the rise of powerful elites and a world of haves and have-nots.

16 It can be inferred from paragraph 4 that prior to the development of agriculture, there
- Ⓐ was great equality among people
- Ⓑ was a class of leaders in most groups
- Ⓒ were some types of craftsmen
- Ⓓ were no conflicts among humans

17 The word "perpetrated" in the passage is closest in meaning to
- Ⓐ caused
- Ⓑ damaged
- Ⓒ happened
- Ⓓ committed

18 According to paragraph 5, centers of urbanization in all ages
- Ⓐ have developed only in places of agricultural development
- Ⓑ have attracted the best and brightest people
- Ⓒ have been responsible for the spread of disease
- Ⓓ have had problems that are similar to one another

With a surplus of food available, people had time to take part in activities other than food procurement. Artisans, merchants, scholars, engineers, priests, bureaucrats, permanent garrisons, and a myriad of others were fed by the surplus labor of the masses. ■ For the first time in human history, a distinction grew between different groups of people: those who grew the food and those who did not. ■ Perversely, those who did not grow the food became more powerful by using their free time to plan cities and temples, develop weapons, gather armies, and wage war on their fellow humans. ■ The masses of people became tied to the land and labored for the few elites at the top. ■

19 Look at the four squares [■] that indicate where the following sentence could be added to the passage.

War had existed before man moved into cities, but after the development of agriculture and urbanization, it became more organized and deadlier.

Where would the sentence best fit?

Click on a square [■] to add the sentence to the passage.

20 Directions: An introductory sentence for a brief summary of the passage is provided below. Complete the summary by selecting the THREE answer choices that express the most important ideas of the passage. Some sentences do not belong because they express ideas that are not presented in the passage or are minor ideas in the passage. **This question is worth 2 points.**

Drag your answer choices to the spaces where they belong.
To remove an answer choice, click on it. To review the passage, click on **View Text**.

The development of agriculture is directly linked to the urbanization of humanity.

-
-
-

Answer Choices

1. Crops were vulnerable to destruction, so it was necessary to live near them to protect them, which gave rise to permanent settlements.

2. The original centers of agriculture and urbanization spread all over the world and cultivated the wild plants found in their natural surroundings.

3. The skills necessary for planting, harvesting, and storing food were acquired over the centuries, which made it possible to have food surpluses.

4. The differences between those with the power to command others and those who did work were more obvious with the spread of agriculture and urbanization.

5. Ultimately, urbanization led to increases in crime, the spread of disease, and a lowering of human moral values, conditions which persist to this day.

6. The rise of elite societies with time to develop skills other than food procurement enabled man to progress at an incredible speed.

How to Master Skills for the TOEFL® iBT

Actual Test
READING 2

03

TOEFL READING

Reading Section Directions

This section measures your ability to understand academic passages in English. You will have **35 minutes** to read and answer questions about **2 passages**. A clock at the top of the screen will show you how much time is remaining.

Most questions are worth 1 point but the last question for each passage is worth more than 1 point. The directions for the last question indicate how many points you may receive.

Some passages include a word or phrase that is **underlined** in blue. Click on the word or phrase to see a definition or an explanation.

When you want to move to the next question, click on **Next**. You may skip questions and go back to them later. If you want to return to previous questions, click on **Back**. You can click on **Review** at any time, and the review screen will show you which questions you have answered and which you have not answered. From this review screen, you may go directly to any question you have already seen in the Reading section.

Click on **Continue** to go on.

Periodic Discoveries

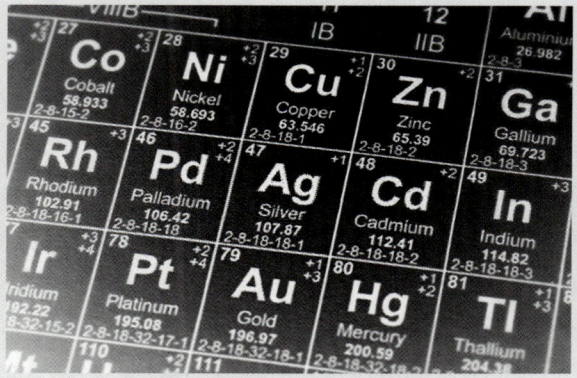

A section of the periodic table

The periodic table of the elements allows chemists and other scientists to view a systematic organization of the elements that make up the universe. When scientists first developed the table in the nineteenth century, they discovered that their methods of organization meant that there were some missing elements that were, as yet, unknown to man. It can be argued that the very development of the table itself led science down the path toward discovering these elements to the point where it is now possible for man to create new elements. This process was one of trial and error and took great advances in theory and technology before humans reached the point where they are today. Even now, chemists are expanding the periodic table.

There are ninety-four known elements that exist in a natural state. Of these, only twelve were known prior to the eighteenth century. These included carbon, iron, and the rare metals silver and gold. By the end of the eighteenth century, there were eighty known elements, and scientists had begun searching for ways to organize them. Men of knowledge in ancient Greece had proposed the atomic theory of element structure, and this was revived and used to organize the elements by utilizing the elements' atomic weights as focal points. Johann Dobereiner, a German chemist, noticed that with certain elements, when grouped in threes, the atomic weight of one fell exactly halfway between the atomic weight of the other two. Based on this, in 1829, he proposed the Law of Triads, which led other chemists to take up the challenge of organizing the elements and to notice that similar characteristics also occurred with groups of eight elements.

All this was the **precursor** to the work of famed Russian chemist Dmitri Mendeleev, who is considered the father of the periodic table. Mendeleev decided to write down all the information he had concerning each element on a separate card and then arranged the cards according to similar characteristics. When the cards were arranged, Mendeleev realized that several elements were missing from the repeating patterns and concluded that there must be unknown elements. He deliberately left spaces in his table to show where they could be placed. It was not until the twentieth century, when new theories of atomic structure were proposed and proven, including the assigning of an atomic number based on the number of protons in an atom, that the table became more complete. When the elements were organized according to atomic number, Mendeleev's table made more sense. Even so, it was not a perfect picture of repeated patterns. One of the things that did not quite fit the table's repeated patterns were the rare earth elements, which had atomic numbers from 57 to 71. They are often placed below the table in a separate row for themselves.

The search for new elements began in earnest and was given a boost by the creation of the atomic reactor and the particle accelerator for the atomic bomb project during World War II. One of the discoveries that came out of this research was element 94, plutonium, the element used in most of the world's nuclear weapons. American Glenn Seaborg found it in 1940 and also had a hand in creating elements 95 to 102 in the 1940s and 1950s. He even has element 106, seaborgium, named for him, and he is responsible for much of the way the periodic table is organized today. The table suggested that elements could be found or created with atomic numbers up to 153, but so far, chemists have only reached number 118. Many of these have only been created for a brief time in very specifically controlled environments, and some are presently doubted by the scientific community.

It can clearly be seen that the drive to organize the elements into a systematic pattern allowed scientists to see that other elements were possible, whether in nature or created by man. Coupled with this were the new theories of atomic structure and the development of technology that has allowed man to discover and create previously unknown elements. Whether or not this is for the good of humanity is yet to be seen.

Glossary
precursor: something leading up to another thing later in time

Periodic Discoveries

1 → The periodic table of the elements allows chemists and other scientists to view a systematic organization of the elements that make up the universe. When scientists first developed the table in the nineteenth century, they discovered that their methods of organization meant that there were some missing elements that were, as yet, unknown to man. It can be argued that the very development of the table itself led science down the path toward discovering these elements to the point where it is now possible for man to create new elements. This process was one of trial and error and took great advances in theory and technology before humans reached the point where they are today. Even now, chemists are expanding the periodic table.

1 According to paragraph 1, the search for the missing elements of the periodic table has been

Ⓐ accomplished easily and in a short period of time
Ⓑ an ongoing process since the nineteenth century
Ⓒ full of obstacles and periodic setbacks
Ⓓ so successful that the table is now complete

2 → There are ninety-four known elements that exist in a natural state. Of these, only twelve were known prior to the eighteenth century. These included carbon, iron, and the rare metals silver and gold. By the end of the eighteenth century, there were eighty known elements, and scientists had begun searching for ways to organize them. Men of knowledge in ancient Greece had proposed the atomic theory of element structure, and this was revived and used to organize the elements by utilizing the elements' atomic weights as focal points. Johann Dobereiner, a German chemist, noticed that with certain elements, when grouped in threes, the atomic weight of one fell exactly halfway between the atomic weight of the other two. Based on this, in 1829, he proposed the Law of Triads, which led other chemists to take up the challenge of organizing the elements and to notice that similar characteristics also occurred with groups of eight elements.

2. According to paragraph 2, which of the following is NOT true of the elements?

   A) Very few were known prior to the 1700s.
   B) Not all of the elements occur naturally on the Earth.
   C) Some of them can be grouped by similar properties.
   D) The atomic theory of elements is a modern idea.

³ → All this was the **precursor** to the work of famed Russian chemist Dmitri Mendeleev, who is considered the father of the periodic table. Mendeleev decided to write down all the information he had concerning each element on a separate card and then arranged the cards according to similar characteristics. When the cards were arranged, Mendeleev realized that several elements were missing from the repeating patterns and concluded that there must be unknown elements. He deliberately left spaces in his table to show where they could be placed. It was not until the twentieth century, when new theories of atomic structure were proposed and proven, including the assigning of an atomic number based on the number of protons in an atom, that the table became more complete. When the elements were organized according to atomic number, Mendeleev's table made more sense. Even so, it was not a perfect picture of repeated patterns. One of the things that did not quite fit the table's repeated patterns were the rare earth elements, which had atomic numbers from 57 to 71. They are often placed below the table in a separate row for themselves.

📖 *Glossary*

precursor: something leading up to another thing later in time

3. The word "They" in the passage refers to
   Ⓐ The things
   Ⓑ The table's repeated patterns
   Ⓒ The rare earth elements
   Ⓓ Atomic numbers

4. According to paragraph 3, which of the following is true of Mendeleev's periodic table?
   Ⓐ It was not as good as those developed by earlier scientists.
   Ⓑ It was able to recognize how new elements could be found.
   Ⓒ It was imperfect but a great advancement in chemistry.
   Ⓓ It was the reason the theory of atomic structure was revised.

4 → The search for new elements began in earnest and was given a boost by the creation of the atomic reactor and the particle accelerator for the atomic bomb project during World War II. One of the discoveries that came out of this research was element 94, plutonium, the element used in most of the world's nuclear weapons. American Glenn Seaborg found it in 1940 and also had a hand in creating elements 95 to 102 in the 1940s and 1950s. He even has element 106, seaborgium, named for him, and he is responsible for much of the way the periodic table is organized today. The table suggested that elements could be found or created with atomic numbers up to 153, but so far, chemists have only reached number 118. Many of these have only been created for a brief time in very specifically controlled environments, and some are presently doubted by the scientific community.

5. Which of the sentences below best expresses the essential information in the highlighted sentence in the passage? *Incorrect* answer choices change the meaning in important ways or leave out essential information.
   A. The atomic bomb project prevented the search for new elements from making progress.
   B. The search for new elements was aided by the atomic bomb project's technological advances.
   C. The discovery of new elements made it possible to create the technology for the atomic bomb project.
   D. The atomic bomb project was necessary for the discovery of new elements.

6. In paragraph 4, the author discusses "American Glenn Seaborg" in order to
   A. admit that he is a controversial figure in chemistry
   B. argue that he was not responsible for some manmade elements
   C. praise him for the work he did with natural elements
   D. describe his contributions to the field of chemistry

7. According to paragraph 4, some of the recently discovered and created elements
   A. are not yet fully accepted as actual facts
   B. can be created for long periods of time
   C. are named after famous scientists
   D. cannot be seen without special equipment

It can clearly be seen that the drive to organize the elements into a systematic pattern allowed scientists to see that other elements were possible, whether in nature or created by man. Coupled with this were the new theories of atomic structure and the development of technology that has allowed man to discover and create previously unknown elements. Whether or not this is for the good of humanity is yet to be seen.

8. The word "previously" in the passage is closest in meaning to
   A. lately
   B. earlier
   C. after
   D. sooner

All this was the **precursor** to the work of famed Russian chemist Dmitri Mendeleev, who is considered the father of the periodic table. Mendeleev decided to write down all the information he had concerning each element on a separate card and then arranged the cards according to similar characteristics. When the cards were arranged, Mendeleev realized that several elements were missing from the repeating patterns and concluded that there must be unknown elements. ■1 He deliberately left spaces in his table to show where they could be placed. ■2 It was not until the twentieth century, when new theories of atomic structure were proposed and proven, including the assigning of an atomic number based on the number of protons in an atom, that the table became more complete. ■3 When the elements were organized according to atomic number, Mendeleev's table made more sense. ■4 Even so, it was not a perfect picture of repeated patterns. One of the things that did not quite fit the table's repeated patterns were the rare earth elements, which had atomic numbers from 57 to 71. They are often placed below the table in a separate row for themselves.

9. Look at the four squares [■] that indicate where the following sentence could be added to the passage.

   The protons carried a positive electric charge, and their number remained constant, meaning they were useful for organizing the elements.

   Where would the sentence best fit?

   Click on a square [■] to add the sentence to the passage.

Glossary

precursor: something leading up to another thing later in time

10 Directions: An introductory sentence for a brief summary of the passage is provided below. Complete the summary by selecting the THREE answer choices that express the most important ideas of the passage. Some sentences do not belong because they express ideas that are not presented in the passage or are minor ideas in the passage. **This question is worth 2 points.**

Drag your answer choices to the spaces where they belong.
To remove an answer choice, click on it. To review the passage, click on **View Text**.

Many people contributed to discoveries that created the periodic table of the elements.

-
-
-

Answer Choices

1. Many new elements were created by humans in the years after World War II ended.

2. Dmitri Mendeleev is primarily responsible for the creation of the periodic table of the elements.

3. Most of the elements on the periodic table were discovered in the years after 1700.

4. Chemists believe that there may be a total of 153 different elements that can exist.

5. One of the elements on the periodic table has been named after Glenn Seaborg.

6. The Law of Triads made by Johann Dobereiner helped with the arrangement of elements on the periodic table.

The Panama Canal

Closed lock gates at Gatun Locks, Panama Canal

While the Panama Canal remains one of the greatest human achievements in history, its locks and canals were not built overnight. Its ultimate completion in 1914 was the result of decades of planning, preparation, and construction, not to mention loss of human life. Two countries, France and the United States, were the main players in its construction, and both faced numerous hardships during the project. There were so many hardships that France, the instigator of the project, eventually had to sell out to the United States, the country that finally completed the canal. Still, the United States faced a trio of major hurdles that threatened its completion. These obstacles were political, environmental, and geographical. Yet through perseverance and will, the United States was ultimately able to create the canal, a vital link between the Pacific and Atlantic oceans.

One of the major reasons France abandoned the Panama Canal project was that it underestimated the environs of the local area. The region of Panama within which the French worked was a dense tropical jungle. Intense heat and humidity did not help their situation either. Before long, many workers began succumbing to diseases like yellow fever and malaria. Proper measures were not taken to reduce their exposure and vulnerability, and many died as the workforce and the entire project suffered greatly. However, once the Americans assumed command of the canal project, they immediately implemented better living conditions and infrastructure for the workforce, including better healthcare facilities. With a stronger workforce and a more extensive healthcare system in place, the Americans stood a better chance of completing the project than the French.

But before the United States could continue with the canal project the French had begun, it had to receive permission from Colombia. At the time, Panama was within the borders of Colombia. President Theodore Roosevelt offered the Colombian government ten million dollars, which it immediately rejected. Ever patient, Roosevelt did not press the issue, and before long, the Panamanians revolted against Colombia for independence. This gave Roosevelt the opportunity he had been waiting for. He immediately sent a substantial military presence to the area to guarantee Panama's independence and to ensure the future construction of the Panama Canal. With Panama free, the door was open for the Americans to continue building a canal, which would save 18,000 miles on a trip from San Francisco to New York and open trade in the Pacific realm.

Once the United States got its hands on the area, the next immediate issue was a geological obstacle. While the verdant hills of Panama looked benign enough, the diversity and makeup of the underlying sediment made it an engineering nightmare. Initially, landslides regularly destroyed weeks or even months of digging and construction as they did to the French. Yet in a stroke of engineering brilliance, through the implementation of a system of dams, this issue was reduced and all but alleviated. Additionally, as the tidal levels of the Pacific and Atlantic were vastly different, a new canal system, unlike the sea-level canal attempted by the French, had to be erected. American engineers decided to install a system of locks to raise and lower ships to the designated sea level. The way in which they could manipulate water helped the Americans overcome the tough geological conditions which had thwarted the French.

Once completed, the Panama Canal stretched for fifty-one miles across Central America and connected the Pacific and Atlantic oceans through sheer human ingenuity and patience. The canal opened endless new possibilities for trade and commerce between Asia and the Americas, which still exist today. But the canal did not come about without severe difficulties and tragedy. It took two countries two separate attempts and over twenty years of backbreaking labor to achieve. One country, France, had to pack up and go home in failure. The other, the United States, could relish the milestone it had achieved. Still, in the end, more than thirty thousand men lost their lives directly or indirectly in the building of the Panama Canal, which proves once and for all what a monumental task it truly was, especially for the age in which it was attempted.

The Panama Canal

1 → While the Panama Canal remains one of the greatest human achievements in history, its locks and canals were not built overnight. Its ultimate completion in 1914 was the result of decades of planning, preparation, and construction, not to mention loss of human life. Two countries, France and the United States, were the main players in its construction, and both faced numerous hardships during the project. There were so many hardships that France, the instigator of the project, eventually had to sell out to the United States, the country that finally completed the canal. Still, the United States faced a trio of major hurdles that threatened its completion. These obstacles were political, environmental, and geographical. Yet through perseverance and will, the United States was ultimately able to create the canal, a vital link between the Pacific and Atlantic oceans.

11 The word "perseverance" in the passage is closest in meaning to
- (A) determination
- (B) procrastination
- (C) cooperation
- (D) precision

12 According to paragraph 1, which of the following is true of the Panama Canal?
- (A) It was finally completed in the first decade of the twentieth century.
- (B) The United States and France worked in unison on its construction.
- (C) The original construction of the canal faced few difficult issues.
- (D) The United States eventually purchased the project from France.

² → One of the major reasons France abandoned the Panama Canal project was that it underestimated the environs of the local area. The region of Panama within which the French worked was a dense tropical jungle. Intense heat and humidity did not help their situation either. Before long, many workers began succumbing to diseases like yellow fever and malaria. Proper measures were not taken to reduce their exposure and vulnerability, and many died as the workforce and the entire project suffered greatly. However, once the Americans assumed command of the canal project, they immediately implemented better living conditions and infrastructure for the workforce, including better healthcare facilities. With a stronger workforce and a more extensive healthcare system in place, the Americans stood a better chance of completing the project than the French.

13 Which of the following can be inferred from paragraph 2 about the Americans?

Ⓐ They tried to prevent the laborers from deserting the construction sites.

Ⓑ They destroyed the dense jungle first to eliminate any diseases.

Ⓒ They were able to learn from the shortcomings that had affected France.

Ⓓ They were not prepared for the punishing climate in Central America.

³→ But before the United States could continue with the canal project the French had begun, it had to receive permission from Colombia. At the time, Panama was within the borders of Colombia. President Theodore Roosevelt offered the Colombian government ten million dollars, which it immediately rejected. Ever patient, Roosevelt did not press the issue, and before long, the Panamanians revolted against Colombia for independence. This gave Roosevelt the opportunity he had been waiting for. He immediately sent a substantial military presence to the area to guarantee Panama's independence and to ensure the future construction of the Panama Canal. With Panama free, the door was open for the Americans to continue building a canal, which would save 18,000 miles on a trip from San Francisco to New York and open trade in the Pacific realm.

14 According to paragraph 3, politics became a problem because

Ⓐ Roosevelt was not aggressive enough when dealing with the canal

Ⓑ The presence of the U.S. military frightened many of the workers

Ⓒ Panama wished to remain a territory of the country of Colombia

Ⓓ Colombia did not wish to give up the rights to the land for the canal

4 → Once the United States got its hands on the area, the next immediate issue was a geological obstacle. While the verdant hills of Panama looked benign enough, the diversity and makeup of the underlying sediment made it an engineering nightmare. Initially, landslides regularly destroyed weeks or even months of digging and construction as they did to the French. Yet in a stroke of engineering brilliance, through the implementation of a system of dams, this issue was reduced and all but alleviated. Additionally, as the tidal levels of the Pacific and Atlantic were vastly different, a new canal system, unlike the sea-level canal attempted by the French, had to be erected. American engineers decided to install a system of locks to raise and lower ships to the designated sea level. The way in which they could manipulate water helped the Americans overcome the tough geological conditions which had thwarted the French.

5 → Once completed, the Panama Canal stretched for fifty-one miles across Central America and connected the Pacific and Atlantic oceans through sheer human ingenuity and patience. The canal opened endless new possibilities for trade and commerce between Asia and the Americas, which still exist today. But the canal did not come about without severe difficulties and tragedy. It took two countries two separate attempts and over twenty years of backbreaking labor to achieve. One country, France, had to pack up and go home in failure. The other, the United States, could relish the milestone it had achieved. Still, in the end, more than thirty thousand men lost their lives directly or indirectly in the building of the Panama Canal, which proves once and for all what a monumental task it truly was, especially for the age in which it was attempted.

15 The author discusses "a geological obstacle" in paragraph 4 in order to

Ⓐ note the natural beauty of Panama, which was destroyed by the canal's construction
Ⓑ suggest that the workers had to spend a lot of time and effort on reconstruction
Ⓒ contrast the geological issues with the oceanic ones the engineers of the project faced
Ⓓ show how landslides were more of a problem for the French than they were for the Americans

16 According to paragraphs 4 and 5, which of the following is NOT true of the construction of the Panama Canal?

Ⓐ It suffered setbacks that cost many months of work due to various problems with the land.
Ⓑ It incorporated dams to accelerate the construction process, which helped make it successful.
Ⓒ It took more than two decades and work by two countries in order to be completed.
Ⓓ It was easier to achieve because of the similar tidal levels of the Pacific and Atlantic Oceans.

5 → Once completed, the Panama Canal stretched for fifty-one miles across Central America and connected the Pacific and Atlantic oceans through sheer human ingenuity and patience. The canal opened endless new possibilities for trade and commerce between Asia and the Americas, which still exist today. But the canal did not come about without severe difficulties and tragedy. It took two countries two separate attempts and over twenty years of backbreaking labor to achieve. One country, France, had to pack up and go home in failure. The other, the United States, could relish the milestone it had achieved. Still, in the end, more than thirty thousand men lost their lives directly or indirectly in the building of the Panama Canal, which proves once and for all what a monumental task it truly was, especially for the age in which it was attempted.

17 Which of the sentences below best expresses the essential information in the highlighted sentence in the passage? *Incorrect* answer choices change the meaning in important ways or leave out essential information.

- (A) Tens of thousands of men died during the construction of the Panama Canal.
- (B) Though the project caused many fatalities, it stands as a lofty achievement.
- (C) The Panama Canal could have been completed later with less loss of life.
- (D) Men were killed on the job and by residual effects such as disease and injury.

18 According to paragraph 5, the completion of the Panama Canal

- (A) created a forty-one-mile link between the Atlantic and Pacific oceans
- (B) helped allow for greater economic benefit between the East and the West
- (C) took much longer than originally planned by the first French engineers
- (D) resulted from the United States having better funding than the French

One of the major reasons France abandoned the Panama Canal project was that it underestimated the environs of the local area. The region of Panama within which the French worked was a dense tropical jungle. Intense heat and humidity did not help their situation either. ■ Before long, many workers began succumbing to diseases like yellow fever and malaria. ■ Proper measures were not taken to reduce their exposure and vulnerability, and many died as the workforce and the entire project suffered greatly. ■ However, once the Americans assumed command of the canal project, they immediately implemented better living conditions and infrastructure for the workforce, including better healthcare facilities. ■ With a stronger workforce and a more extensive healthcare system in place, the Americans stood a better chance of completing the project than the French.

19 Look at the four squares [■] that indicate where the following sentence could be added to the passage.

In contrast, France erected only one tiny field hospital for all of its sick employees.

Where would the sentence best fit?

Click on a square [■] to add the sentence to the passage.

20 Directions: An introductory sentence for a brief summary of the passage is provided below. Complete the summary by selecting the THREE answer choices that express the most important ideas of the passage. Some sentences do not belong because they express ideas that are not presented in the passage or are minor ideas in the passage. **This question is worth 2 points.**

Drag your answer choices to the spaces where they belong.
To remove an answer choice, click on it. To review the passage, click on **View Text**.

The construction of the Panama Canal, though difficult and full of hardships, created a vital link between the Pacific and Atlantic oceans.

-
-
-

Answer Choices

1. France first began the project but eventually left it for the United States to complete.

2. Disease was one of the major obstacles that France was not able to overcome.

3. By employing dam and lock systems, the Americans were able to be successful.

4. The Panama Canal stretches for over fifteen miles between the Pacific and the Atlantic.

5. Roosevelt was empathetic toward the Panamanians and their desire for freedom.

6. Though the French created many hospitals, men were stricken with illness and injury.

How to Master Skills for the TOEFL® iBT

Actual Test
READING 2

04

TOEFL READING

Reading Section Directions

This section measures your ability to understand academic passages in English. You will have **35 minutes** to read and answer questions about **2 passages**. A clock at the top of the screen will show you how much time is remaining.

Most questions are worth 1 point but the last question for each passage is worth more than 1 point. The directions for the last question indicate how many points you may receive.

Some passages include a word or phrase that is **underlined** in blue. Click on the word or phrase to see a definition or an explanation.

When you want to move to the next question, click on **Next**. You may skip questions and go back to them later. If you want to return to previous questions, click on **Back**. You can click on **Review** at any time, and the review screen will show you which questions you have answered and which you have not answered. From this review screen, you may go directly to any question you have already seen in the Reading section.

Click on **Continue** to go on.

Invasive Fish

A close-up view of a clearfin lionfish

  Most plants and animals live in specific habitats, where they become integral parts of their ecosystems and live together well with the other plants and animals there. At times, a new plant or animal may be introduced to an ecosystem in which it does not normally live. This is known as an exotic species. As time passes, some exotic species begin to reproduce in their new ecosystems as they establish themselves there, at which point they become known as invasive species. As a general rule, invasive species, of which there are many fish, can be highly disruptive and may cause numerous problems to the environment, the economy, and the health of other species in their new ecosystems.

  Invasive fish can be found in saltwater locations such as oceans, seas, gulfs, and bays as well as in freshwater waterways such as rivers, lakes, streams, ponds, and creeks. They may dwell in water that is just a few inches deep to water that descends thousands of feet beneath the ocean's surface. One recent study of thousands of rivers around the world determined that there were approximately 500 species of invasive fish living in them, and the researchers believed they had not found every species of fish living where they were not supposed to be.

  One of the problems with invasive fish is that they frequently have no natural predators in their new ecosystems, which makes it easy for them to reproduce and quickly to increase their numbers. As a result, they often begin outcompeting the native fish for valuable food resources. This, in turn, can cause the numbers of native fish to decline, which frequently upsets the balance in various ecosystems. Many invasive fish, such as snakeheads, are extreme predators with voracious appetites. These fish, some of which are capable of breathing air and walking from pond to pond, can devour all of the fish in a pond quickly, especially because a single snakehead can produce thousands of eggs in a single year. Invasive fish such as snakeheads can therefore reduce the amount of biological diversity in some places.

Another invasive fish is the lionfish. Native to the tropical waters of the Indian and Pacific oceans, this fish has taken over warm areas in the Atlantic Ocean, the Caribbean Sea, and the Gulf of Mexico. Much like the snakehead, the lionfish is a predator with an enormous appetite and is additionally capable of reproducing quickly. Another feature of the lionfish is that it is a venomous fish that can cause serious harm to humans at times. Much of the damage done by lionfish is economic in nature. First, it feeds on fish that are of commercial value to humans and has reduced the numbers of those fish, meaning that fishermen are catching few of them these days. Another factor is that lionfish can often be found in coral reefs, which are renowned for the diversity of life they feature. However, lionfish have reduced the numbers of various fish in coral reefs, so many scuba divers interested in seeing different fish have stopped visiting those reefs. This causes economic harm to the people whose livelihoods depend on coral reefs.

Most invasive fish arrive at new destinations because of human actions. For instance, people sometimes become tired of caring for fish in their **aquariums**, so they may release these fish into the wild. Occasionally, fish farmed for **aquaculture** may escape and get into the wild; likewise, live fish that scientists conduct research upon have also been known to escape and get into places where they should not be. As humans are responsible for these invasive fish, it is only right that humans take action to remove them, too. Fishermen who catch snakeheads are urged not to release them but to kill them and to alert authorities regarding where they were caught. Likewise, scuba divers are asked to catch or kill lionfish. There is even an effort to popularize eating these fish, which will make more people willing to catch them. With luck, the populations of invasive fish such as snakeheads and lionfish will be reduced, and their ecosystems will be returned to their prior conditions.

Glossary
aquarium: a tank in which fish or other marine animals are kept
aquaculture: the act of fish farming

Invasive Fish

1 → Most plants and animals live in specific habitats, where they become integral parts of their ecosystems and live together well with the other plants and animals there. At times, a new plant or animal may be introduced to an ecosystem in which it does not normally live. This is known as an exotic species. As time passes, some exotic species begin to reproduce in their new ecosystems as they establish themselves there, at which point they become known as invasive species. As a general rule, invasive species, of which there are many fish, can be highly disruptive and may cause numerous problems to the environment, the economy, and the health of other species in their new ecosystems.

1. In paragraph 1, why does the author mention "an exotic species"?
   - Ⓐ To claim that exotic species can be found everywhere
   - Ⓑ To point out some of the harm exotic species can cause
   - Ⓒ To argue that exotic species can benefit some ecosystems
   - Ⓓ To contrast its definition with that of an invasive species

2. The word "disruptive" in the passage is closest in meaning to
   - Ⓐ troublesome
   - Ⓑ reproductive
   - Ⓒ apparent
   - Ⓓ dangerous

2 → Invasive fish can be found in saltwater locations such as oceans, seas, gulfs, and bays as well as in freshwater waterways such as rivers, lakes, streams, ponds, and creeks. They may dwell in water that is just a few inches deep to water that descends thousands of feet beneath the ocean's surface. One recent study of thousands of rivers around the world determined that there were approximately 500 species of invasive fish living in them, and the researchers believed they had not found every species of fish living where they were not supposed to be.

3. Which of the sentences below best expresses the essential information in the highlighted sentence in the passage? *Incorrect* answer choices change the meaning in important ways or leave out essential information.

   A. Many invasive fish move from saltwater locations to freshwater waterways.
   B. There are invasive fish living in both freshwater and saltwater environments.
   C. More invasive fish live in fresh water than are found in salt water.
   D. Ocean, seas, and other saltwater locations have large numbers of invasive fish.

4. Which of the following can be inferred from paragraph 2 about invasive fish?

   A. There are more than 500 species of invasive fish in the Earth's rivers.
   B. They have caused some native species of fish to become extinct.
   C. Most of them are found deep in the oceans rather than in rivers.
   D. Some of them reproduce so quickly that they cause native fish to die out.

³→ One of the problems with invasive fish is that they frequently have no natural predators in their new ecosystems, which makes it easy for them to reproduce and quickly to increase their numbers. As a result, they often begin outcompeting the native fish for valuable food resources. This, in turn, can cause the numbers of native fish to decline, which frequently upsets the balance in various ecosystems. Many invasive fish, such as snakeheads, are extreme predators with voracious appetites. These fish, some of which are capable of breathing air and walking from pond to pond, can devour all of the fish in a pond quickly, especially because a single snakehead can produce thousands of eggs in a single year. Invasive fish such as snakeheads can therefore reduce the amount of biological diversity in some places.

5. In paragraph 3, the author's description of native fish mentions which of the following?
   Ⓐ The names of several species of them
   Ⓑ Where on the Earth they are the most common
   Ⓒ The sizes some of them can grow to be
   Ⓓ How they can make ecosystems unbalanced

⁴ ➜ Another invasive fish is the lionfish. Native to the tropical waters of the Indian and Pacific oceans, this fish has taken over warm areas in the Atlantic Ocean, the Caribbean Sea, and the Gulf of Mexico. Much like the snakehead, the lionfish is a predator with an enormous appetite and is additionally capable of reproducing quickly. Another feature of the lionfish is that it is a venomous fish that can cause serious harm to humans at times. Much of the damage done by lionfish is economic in nature. First, it feeds on fish that are of commercial value to humans and has reduced the numbers of those fish, meaning that fishermen are catching few of them these days. Another factor is that lionfish can often be found in coral reefs, which are renowned for the diversity of life they feature. However, lionfish have reduced the numbers of various fish in coral reefs, so many scuba divers interested in seeing different fish have stopped visiting those reefs. This causes economic harm to the people whose livelihoods depend on coral reefs.

6 In paragraph 4, all of the following questions are answered EXCEPT:

Ⓐ How are lionfish harming the economies of some places?

Ⓑ How does lionfish venom affect humans?

Ⓒ Why are lionfish causing commercial fish numbers to decline?

Ⓓ Which places have lionfish invaded and now live in?

7 The word "they" refers to

Ⓐ humans

Ⓑ fishermen

Ⓒ lionfish

Ⓓ coral reefs

5 → Most invasive fish arrive at new destinations because of human actions. For instance, people sometimes become tired of caring for fish in their **aquariums**, so they may release these fish into the wild. Occasionally, fish farmed for **aquaculture** may escape and get into the wild; likewise, live fish that scientists conduct research upon have also been known to escape and get into places where they should not be. As humans are responsible for these invasive fish, it is only right that humans take action to remove them, too. Fishermen who catch snakeheads are urged not to release them but to kill them and to alert authorities regarding where they were caught. Likewise, scuba divers are asked to catch or kill lionfish. There is even an effort to popularize eating these fish, which will make more people willing to catch them. With luck, the populations of invasive fish such as snakeheads and lionfish will be reduced, and their ecosystems will be returned to their prior conditions.

8. According to paragraph 5, the numbers of invasive fish can be reduced by
   Ⓐ killing any invasive fish that are caught
   Ⓑ spreading poison in their breeding grounds
   Ⓒ trying to catch as many females as possible
   Ⓓ using nets to catch large numbers of them

Glossary
aquarium: a tank in which fish or other marine animals are kept
aquaculture: the act of fish farming

One of the problems with invasive fish is that they frequently have no natural predators in their new ecosystems, which makes it easy for them to reproduce and quickly to increase their numbers. As a result, they often begin outcompeting the native fish for valuable food resources. This, in turn, can cause the numbers of native fish to decline, which frequently upsets the balance in various ecosystems. **[1]** Many invasive fish, such as snakeheads, are extreme predators with voracious appetites. **[2]** These fish, some of which are capable of breathing air and walking from pond to pond, can devour all of the fish in a pond quickly, especially because a single snakehead can produce thousands of eggs in a single year. **[3]** Invasive fish such as snakeheads can therefore reduce the amount of biological diversity in some places. **[4]**

9. Look at the four squares [■] that indicate where the following sentence could be added to the passage.

   For instance, ponds with ten species of fish can be reduced to a single species within a year once a snakehead infestation occurs.

   Where would the sentence best fit?

   Click on a square [■] to add the sentence to the passage.

10 Directions: An introductory sentence for a brief summary of the passage is provided below. Complete the summary by selecting the THREE answer choices that express the most important ideas of the passage. Some sentences do not belong because they express ideas that are not presented in the passage or are minor ideas in the passage. **This question is worth 2 points.**

Drag your answer choices to the spaces where they belong.
To remove an answer choice, click on it. To review the passage, click on **View Text**.

Invasive fish cause problems for people and animals around the world.

-
-
-

Answer Choices

1. People are responsible for bringing fish to places where they do not belong.
2. Invasive fish may outcompete native fish for food and other resources.
3. Lionfish harm economies by reducing fish populations in coral reefs.
4. Tropical fish in aquariums may be released into the wild by their owners.
5. Snakeheads can rapidly eliminate other species of fish in ponds.
6. The numbers of some invasive fish have been reduced in certain areas.

The Opening of Japan

Japan in the mid-nineteenth century was a shadow of the modern economic **juggernaut** that is now one of the world's leading traders. For hundreds of years, Japan had been secluded from the outside world by the strict policies of its rulers, the Tokugawa shoguns. With the exception of one Dutch ship per year at the port of Nagasaki, the Japanese refused to deal with foreign ships or nations. Sailors shipwrecked on Japanese islands were treated harshly and often imprisoned. Passing vessels were refused food, water, and other provisions. With a goal to right these wrongs and to open Japan to trade, in 1853, the United States sent its most capable man, Admiral Matthew Perry, and four warships to open Japan to the world. The consequences of those actions are still being felt today.

In the seventeenth century, the Japanese opened their doors briefly to the Dutch and allowed a trading station and Christian enclave in Nagasaki. Guns were imported as part of this trade, and they were one of the reasons for a great upheaval that engulfed Japan for many decades as a civil war raged between powerful shoguns, or warlords. Finally, Tokugawa emerged as the victor and claimed the lordship of Japan. During these upheavals, the emperor had stood by wielding no power and existed merely as a figurehead. Soon after the civil war, the Japanese abandoned the use of guns and the art of gun making. When Admiral Perry and his fleet arrived in 1853, they were defenseless against his awesome firepower.

Perry had three main purposes when he arrived in Japan: to open the country to American trade, to get an agreement to use Japan as a coaling and provisioning station for American vessels, and to provide guarantees that Japan would aid shipwrecked American sailors. He wished to deal only with the highest officials and rebuffed Japanese attempts to foster lower-level emissaries on him. He sailed away to examine further the coast of Taiwan as a possible coaling station but returned to Japan the following spring in March 1854. This time, under threat of naval bombardment, the Japanese relented and finally signed the Treaty of Kanagawa on March 31, 1854. In addition to the three main items, the Japanese agreed to allow an American consulate to be established. At first, only Nagasaki was open to American trade, but the treaty stipulated that, after five years, other ports would be opened.

The consequences of these events were far reaching for Japan and the world. Within a few years, foreign currency began to flow to Japan, which upset its economy and caused rising inflation. This was a precursor to the fall of the Tokugawa shoguns and the return of the emperor as the leader of Japanese affairs in 1868. The Emperor Meiji, not wanting Japan to be under the heel of the foreigners who now clamored at the open door for pieces of his land, then set a clear path for his nation. Meiji sent sailors to England to learn how to build ships and to fight a modern naval war, invited German army officers to train his soldiers, and made deals with many companies to modernize Japan's industry, transportation, and communications. In fact, the efforts were so successful that by the 1890s, the world began to view Japan as one of the great powers, more so after it defeated both China and Russia on land and at sea in two local wars. The Russian defeat was even more astonishing since the Europeans were unused to losing to those they considered their inferiors.

Japan's rapid industrialization and militarization had dreadful consequences for Asia as Meiji's grandson Hirohito led the nation down the path to world war, which ultimately saw the destruction of much of Japan. The shock of this defeat still echoes through Japanese history, as does the arrival of Perry and his warships, whose efforts opened Japan to the world. Unknowingly, he unleashed a powerful force with the Japanese not willing to be subjugated to foreign domination. In the long run, Japan has become part of the global culture and has offered more to the world than could have ever been imagined when Perry's ships first dropped anchor in the past.

Glossary
juggernaut: something that is very large and powerful

The Opening of Japan

1 → Japan in the mid-nineteenth century was a shadow of the modern economic **juggernaut** that is now one of the world's leading traders. For hundreds of years, Japan had been secluded from the outside world by the strict policies of its rulers, the Tokugawa shoguns. With the exception of one Dutch ship per year at the port of Nagasaki, the Japanese refused to deal with foreign ships or nations. Sailors shipwrecked on Japanese islands were treated harshly and often imprisoned. Passing vessels were refused food, water, and other provisions. With a goal to right these wrongs and to open Japan to trade, in 1853, the United States sent its most capable man, Admiral Matthew Perry, and four warships to open Japan to the world. The consequences of those actions are still being felt today.

Glossary
juggernaut: something that is very large and powerful

11 The word "secluded" in the passage is closest in meaning to
  (A) removed
  (B) hidden
  (C) isolated
  (D) reserved

12 According to paragraph 1, which of the following is NOT true of Japan's dealings with foreigners in the mid-nineteenth century?
  (A) No ships were allowed to visit Japan.
  (B) Shipwrecked sailors were badly treated.
  (C) Ships in need were not helped by Japan.
  (D) Japan had a very limited foreign trade.

2 → In the seventeenth century, the Japanese opened their doors briefly to the Dutch and allowed a trading station and Christian enclave in Nagasaki. Guns were imported as part of this trade, and they were one of the reasons for a great upheaval that engulfed Japan for many decades as a civil war raged between powerful shoguns, or warlords. Finally, Tokugawa emerged as the victor and claimed the lordship of Japan. During these upheavals, the emperor had stood by wielding no power and existed merely as a figurehead. Soon after the civil war, the Japanese abandoned the use of guns and the art of gun making. When Admiral Perry and his fleet arrived in 1853, they were defenseless against his awesome firepower.

13 It can be inferred from paragraph 2 that the Japanese abandoned gun making because guns

Ⓐ were the products of foreigners and thus forbidden

Ⓑ were blamed for helping cause the long civil war

Ⓒ went against the Japanese idea of a warrior

Ⓓ were difficult and expensive to make in Japan

3 → Perry had three main purposes when he arrived in Japan: to open the country to American trade, to get an agreement to use Japan as a coaling and provisioning station for American vessels, and to provide guarantees that Japan would aid shipwrecked American sailors. He wished to deal only with the highest officials and rebuffed Japanese attempts to foster lower-level emissaries on him. He sailed away to examine further the coast of Taiwan as a possible coaling station but returned to Japan the following spring in March 1854. This time, under threat of naval bombardment, the Japanese relented and finally signed the Treaty of Kanagawa on March 31, 1854. In addition to the three main items, the Japanese agreed to allow an American consulate to be established. At first, only Nagasaki was open to American trade, but the treaty stipulated that, after five years, other ports would be opened.

14 According to paragraph 3, Admiral Perry's mission to Japan eventually

- Ⓐ achieved exactly what he wanted
- Ⓑ failed to achieve any concrete objectives
- Ⓒ achieved some but not all of his objectives
- Ⓓ achieved more than he had expected

15 According to paragraph 3, the Treaty of Kanagawa was agreed to by the Japanese

- Ⓐ because they wanted to have relations with the United States
- Ⓑ against their wishes under the threat of force of arms
- Ⓒ in order to gain an advantage over the Americans
- Ⓓ because they realized they could not be secluded forever

⁴→ The consequences of these events were far reaching for Japan and the world. Within a few years, foreign currency began to flow to Japan, which upset its economy and caused rising inflation. This was a precursor to the fall of the Tokugawa shoguns and the return of the emperor as the leader of Japanese affairs in 1868. The Emperor Meiji, not wanting Japan to be under the heel of the foreigners who now clamored at the open door for pieces of his land, then set a clear path for his nation. Meiji sent sailors to England to learn how to build ships and to fight a modern naval war, invited German army officers to train his soldiers, and made deals with many companies to modernize Japan's industry, transportation, and communications. In fact, the efforts were so successful that by the 1890s, the world began to view Japan as one of the great powers, more so after it defeated both China and Russia on land and at sea in two local wars. The Russian defeat was even more astonishing since the Europeans were unused to losing to those they considered their inferiors.

16 The author discusses "The Emperor Meiji" in paragraph 4 in order to

Ⓐ explain how he managed to retain power

Ⓑ show his efforts to modernize Japan

Ⓒ criticize him for abandoning traditional ways

Ⓓ name some of his most important advisors

17 Which of the sentences below best expresses the essential information in the highlighted sentence in the passage? *Incorrect* answer choices change the meaning in important ways or leave out essential information.

Ⓐ Europe was not surprised that the Russians lost since they were inferior to Japan.

Ⓑ The Japanese defeat of Russia was surprising because the Russians were effective at fighting wars.

Ⓒ Defeat against Japan embarrassed the Russians in the eyes of the other European nations.

Ⓓ Europeans usually won wars against non-Europeans, so the Russian defeat was a surprise.

Japan's rapid industrialization and militarization had dreadful consequences for Asia as Meiji's grandson Hirohito led the nation down the path to world war, which ultimately saw the destruction of much of Japan. The shock of this defeat still echoes through Japanese history, as does the arrival of Perry and his warships, whose efforts opened Japan to the world. Unknowingly, he unleashed a powerful force with the Japanese not willing to be subjugated to foreign domination. In the long run, Japan has become part of the global culture and has offered more to the world than could have ever been imagined when Perry's ships first dropped anchor in the past.

18. The word "domination" in the passage is closest in meaning to
    - (A) control
    - (B) law
    - (C) dogma
    - (D) monopoly

The consequences of these events were far reaching for Japan and the world. ■ Within a few years, foreign currency began to flow to Japan, which upset its economy and caused rising inflation. ■ This was a precursor to the fall of the Tokugawa shoguns and the return of the emperor as the leader of Japanese affairs in 1868. ■ The Emperor Meiji, not wanting Japan to be under the heel of the foreigners who now clamored at the open door for pieces of his land, then set a clear path for his nation. ■ Meiji sent sailors to England to learn how to build ships and to fight a modern naval war, invited German army officers to train his soldiers, and made deals with many companies to modernize Japan's industry, transportation, and communications. In fact, the efforts were so successful that by the 1890s, the world began to view Japan as one of the great powers, more so after it defeated both China and Russia on land and at sea in two local wars. The Russian defeat was even more astonishing since the Europeans were unused to losing to those they considered their inferiors.

19. Look at the four squares [■] that indicate where the following sentence could be added to the passage.

This change was not accomplished without bloodshed, however, as the samurai class of warriors resisted all attempts to modernize with the rest of the country, and a minor civil war ended with the defeat of the great warriors.

Where would the sentence best fit?

Click on a square [■] to add the sentence to the passage.

20 Directions: An introductory sentence for a brief summary of the passage is provided below. Complete the summary by selecting the THREE answer choices that express the most important ideas of the passage. Some sentences do not belong because they express ideas that are not presented in the passage or are minor ideas in the passage. **This question is worth 2 points.**

Drag your answer choices to the spaces where they belong.
To remove an answer choice, click on it. To review the passage, click on **View Text**.

The opening of Japan in 1854 had a number of consequences over the next few decades.

-
-
-

Answer Choices

1. Japan allowed the Dutch to trade with them for a short period in the seventeenth century.

2. In the late 1800s, the Emperor Meiji began a process of modernizing Japan.

3. American Admiral Perry took warships to Japan and forced it to sign the Treaty of Kanagawa.

4. Sailors that were shipwrecked in Japan were treated horribly until they could be rescued.

5. Shoguns such as Tokugawa had a great amount of power in Japan for a couple of centuries.

6. Japan became industrialized and militarized quickly and managed to defeat both China and Russia in wars.

How to Master Skills for the TOEFL® iBT

Actual Test
READING 2

05

TOEFL READING

Reading Section Directions

This section measures your ability to understand academic passages in English. You will have **35 minutes** to read and answer questions about **2 passages**. A clock at the top of the screen will show you how much time is remaining.

Most questions are worth 1 point but the last question for each passage is worth more than 1 point. The directions for the last question indicate how many points you may receive.

Some passages include a word or phrase that is **underlined** in blue. Click on the word or phrase to see a definition or an explanation.

When you want to move to the next question, click on **Next**. You may skip questions and go back to them later. If you want to return to previous questions, click on **Back**. You can click on **Review** at any time, and the review screen will show you which questions you have answered and which you have not answered. From this review screen, you may go directly to any question you have already seen in the Reading section.

Click on **Continue** to go on.

Skyscrapers

New York city's skyline with skyscrapers

While in today's modern society, skyscrapers may seem ubiquitous, they are relatively recent phenomena in historical terms. The first ones appeared in Chicago in the late nineteenth century, and the building craze about which city or country has the highest one in the world has never really stopped. The United Arab Emirates currently holds the record with Burj Khalifa standing 2,717 feet tall, but this will surely be broken at some future date as buildings are constructed ever higher. Technology makes this all possible, and steel is the main reason skyscrapers exist. Until the invention of a process to make easily produced yet strong steel, it was impossible to build anything higher than around fifteen stories. Yet steel alone did not enable the construction of higher buildings, and it took a combination of steel, improved **hydraulics**, reinforced concrete, and elevators to make the modern skyscraper possible.

As a building rises higher from the ground, gravity acts as a brake on its progression. The common building materials before the invention of steel were wood, stone, bricks, and then iron. Wood is too weak to support very high structures while stone and brick buildings are massive at the bottom and then have to be progressively smaller and lighter toward the top, or the weight will crush the structure. In ancient times, the Egyptian pyramids were the largest structures with massive blocks placed on top of one another, and the pyramids' shapes perfectly distributed the weight around the enormous base. Iron seemed to be the answer to building higher, but its strength was not equal to the task, and structures often collapsed under their own weight.

It took the invention of steel to allow architects and engineers to fulfill their building fantasies. Steel is basically iron with a carbon content that allows it to have greater strength. Iron ore has too much carbon, and the secret to finding the right balance between carbon and iron to make the best steel was a quest that occupied many minds in many countries over the centuries. Steel was known in ancient and medieval times, but it was cumbersome and time consuming to produce with some methods and extremely expensive with others. Then, in the mid-nineteenth century in the English city of Sheffield, Henry Bessemer perfected a fast, inexpensive way to make strong steel from iron. The Bessemer process of steelmaking became the norm around the world and did not fall out of favor until the 1960s.

Steel had both the strength and the **malleability** to allow people to build higher and higher without the necessity of a huge base as was required in stone and brick buildings. Aesthetically speaking, steel is rather ugly to look at, so stone, brick, glass, and reinforced concrete are used to give a building the shape of the architect's vision. Steel has also found usefulness in reinforced concrete, which is a major building material for buildings, bridges, tunnels, and countless other structures. The strength of steel is what allows skyscrapers to reach higher and higher into the sky. In addition to steel, progress in the fields of hydraulics enabled greater water pressure to be applied to buildings to permit plumbing on the highest floors. No one wants to walk up dozens of floors, so the development of the safety elevator by Elisha Otis in 1857 was a big step toward higher buildings.

Historians consider the Home Insurance Building in Chicago the world's first skyscraper. It was built to ten stories in 1884-85. Although shorter than some masonry buildings, it was the first to use an all-steel frame construction to bear the weight of the floors. Today's modern buildings are technical marvels that attract visitors from around the world to observe their unique designs and to see the views from their highest levels. Their familiar shapes fill the skylines of the world, and others are symbols of their nations, like the Empire State Building in New York and the Petronas Towers of Malaysia. They are the combination of many inventive minds of the nineteenth century, but without the development of strong, dependable steel, the skyscrapers of today would most likely not exist.

Glossary
hydraulics: the field of science that is related to fluids
malleability: the capability of being bent into different shapes

Skyscrapers

¹ ➡ While in today's modern society, skyscrapers may seem ubiquitous, they are relatively recent phenomena in historical terms. The first ones appeared in Chicago in the late nineteenth century, and the building craze about which city or country has the highest one in the world has never really stopped. The United Arab Emirates currently holds the record with Burj Khalifa standing 2,717 feet tall, but this will surely be broken at some future date as buildings are constructed ever higher. Technology makes this all possible, and steel is the main reason skyscrapers exist. Until the invention of a process to make easily produced yet strong steel, it was impossible to build anything higher than around fifteen stories. Yet steel alone did not enable the construction of higher buildings, and it took a combination of steel, improved **hydraulics**, reinforced concrete, and elevators to make the modern skyscraper possible.

1 The word "ubiquitous" in the passage is closest in meaning to
- Ⓐ impressive
- Ⓑ pervasive
- Ⓒ outdated
- Ⓓ gigantic

2 According to paragraph 1, the record for the world's tallest building
- Ⓐ has remained the same for a long time
- Ⓑ is not considered very important
- Ⓒ is never going to change in the future
- Ⓓ will be challenged by other buildings in the future

📕 ***Glossary***
hydraulics: the field of science that is related to fluids

2 → As a building rises higher from the ground, gravity acts as a brake on its progression. The common building materials before the invention of steel were wood, stone, bricks, and then iron. Wood is too weak to support very high structures while stone and brick buildings are massive at the bottom and then have to be progressively smaller and lighter toward the top, or the weight will crush the structure. In ancient times, the Egyptian pyramids were the largest structures with massive blocks placed on top of one another, and the pyramids' shapes perfectly distributed the weight around the enormous base. Iron seemed to be the answer to building higher, but its strength was not equal to the task, and structures often collapsed under their own weight.

3. In paragraph 2, the author mentions "wood, stone, bricks, and then iron" in order to

   A) demonstrate why buildings could not be very high
   B) explain the building methods of previous eras
   C) prove that the Egyptian pyramids were the largest structures
   D) show that these materials were adequate for their times

³ ⟶ It took the invention of steel to allow architects and engineers to fulfill their building fantasies. Steel is basically iron with a carbon content that allows it to have greater strength. Iron ore has too much carbon, and the secret to finding the right balance between carbon and iron to make the best steel was a quest that occupied many minds in many countries over the centuries. Steel was known in ancient and medieval times, but it was cumbersome and time consuming to produce with some methods and extremely expensive with others. Then, in the mid-nineteenth century in the English city of Sheffield, Henry Bessemer perfected a fast, inexpensive way to make strong steel from iron. **The Bessemer process of steelmaking became the norm around the world and did not fall out of favor until the 1960s.**

4. Which of the sentences below best expresses the essential information in the highlighted sentence in the passage? *Incorrect* answer choices change the meaning in important ways or leave out essential information.

   Ⓐ It was not until the 1960s that the Bessemer process was known around the world.
   Ⓑ Steelmaking by the Bessemer process became the international standard by the 1960s.
   Ⓒ The Bessemer process was common around the world until the 1960s.
   Ⓓ Normal steelmaking was out of favor until the Bessemer process in the 1960s.

5. According to paragraph 3, why did it take so long to produce cheap but strong steel?

   Ⓐ Too many people were working on the project.
   Ⓑ It was too expensive to conduct many experiments.
   Ⓒ The right mix of carbon and iron eluded experts.
   Ⓓ It was time consuming and difficult to produce.

⁴ ➜ Steel had both the strength and the **malleability** to allow people to build higher and higher without the necessity of a huge base as was required in stone and brick buildings. Aesthetically speaking, steel is rather ugly to look at, so stone, brick, glass, and reinforced concrete are used to give a building the shape of the architect's vision. Steel has also found usefulness in reinforced concrete, which is a major building material for buildings, bridges, tunnels, and countless other structures. The strength of steel is what allows skyscrapers to reach higher and higher into the sky. In addition to steel, progress in the fields of hydraulics enabled greater water pressure to be applied to buildings to permit plumbing on the highest floors. No one wants to walk up dozens of floors, so the development of the safety elevator by Elisha Otis in 1857 was a big step toward higher buildings.

6 It can be inferred from paragraph 4 that steel

Ⓐ is a component of reinforced concrete
Ⓑ cannot be made into many different shapes
Ⓒ is considered pleasing to the eye
Ⓓ was the final necessity for skyscrapers

7 In paragraph 4, the author's description of hindrances to making higher buildings mentions all of the following EXCEPT:

Ⓐ A lack of material strong enough to support the weight
Ⓑ An efficient means of reaching higher floors
Ⓒ Different ways to make steel appear more beautiful
Ⓓ Useful methods to pump water to higher floors

📘 **Glossary**

malleability: the capability of being bent into different shapes

⁵ ➜ Historians consider the Home Insurance Building in Chicago the world's first skyscraper. It was built to ten stories in 1884-85. Although shorter than some masonry buildings, it was the first to use an all-steel frame construction to bear the weight of the floors. Today's modern buildings are technical marvels that attract visitors from around the world to observe their unique designs and to see the views from their highest levels. Their familiar shapes fill the skylines of the world, and others are symbols of their nations, like the Empire State Building in New York and the Petronas Towers of Malaysia. They are the combination of many inventive minds of the nineteenth century, but without the development of strong, dependable steel, the skyscrapers of today would most likely not exist.

8 According to paragraph 5, the author implies that the first skyscraper

Ⓐ was not the tallest building in the world at that time

Ⓑ was the tallest building in Chicago in the nineteenth century

Ⓒ was constructed with both a steel and iron frame

Ⓓ was the first building to look like a modern skyscraper

Steel had both the strength and the **malleability** to allow people to build higher and higher without the necessity of a huge base as was required in stone and brick buildings. Aesthetically speaking, steel is rather ugly to look at, so stone, brick, glass, and reinforced concrete are used to give a building the shape of the architect's vision. Steel has also found usefulness in reinforced concrete, which is a major building material for buildings, bridges, tunnels, and countless other structures. **[1]** The strength of steel is what allows skyscrapers to reach higher and higher into the sky. **[2]** In addition to steel, progress in the fields of hydraulics enabled greater water pressure to be applied to buildings to permit plumbing on the highest floors. **[3]** No one wants to walk up dozens of floors, so the development of the safety elevator by Elisha Otis in 1857 was a big step toward higher buildings. **[4]**

9. Look at the four squares [■] that indicate where the following sentence could be added to the passage.

   Elevating devices had been around since ancient times, but prior to Otis's invention, they had been considered unreliable for very high structures.

   Where would the sentence best fit?

   Click on a square [■] to add the sentence to the passage.

📖 **Glossary**
malleability: the capability of being bent into different shapes

10 Directions: An introductory sentence for a brief summary of the passage is provided below. Complete the summary by selecting the THREE answer choices that express the most important ideas of the passage. Some sentences do not belong because they express ideas that are not presented in the passage or are minor ideas in the passage. **This question is worth 2 points.**

Drag your answer choices to the spaces where they belong.
To remove an answer choice, click on it. To review the passage, click on **View Text**.

Prior to the late nineteenth century, building height was limited, but new technology allowed the creation of the modern skyscraper.

-
-
-

Answer Choices

1. Buildings made of stone and brick cannot be very high due to their inability to bear very heavy loads.

2. The production of cheap but strong steel provided a building material that could hold the weight of very high buildings.

3. Many people tried to find the secret of the right combination of carbon and iron to make strong yet cheap steel.

4. The invention of the safety elevator and improvements in hydraulic systems permitted comfortable living in high buildings.

5. Many cities around the world want to be known for having the world's tallest building.

6. Glass and reinforced concrete on a frame of steel have allowed the modern architect's vision to become a reality.

The Structure of the Universe

A monument of Nicolaus Copernicus in Torun, Poland

Humans have questioned the creation of the universe since ancient times and have wondered where and how it came into being and what man's location in it was. Religion and science have often clashed in this search with many people willing to believe that a higher being moves the heavens and Earth while others have looked for a physical explanation. In the past, there were many theories as to Earth's position in this universe; the works of Ptolemy and Nicolas Copernicus were the best known. Their theories differed on a very important point: whether Earth or the sun was the center of the universe. Copernicus's theory, enhanced by the works of other famous scientists, is accepted as fact today.

Ptolemy's theory suggested that Earth was the center of the universe and that everything revolved around it. Most of his theory was accepted on faith rather than on scientific proof, especially astronomical and mathematical proof. That Earth should be the center of the known realm of mankind did not clash with religious values, seemed natural, and gave **credence** to the idea that man was master of the universe. This theory was held as evident truth for more than one thousand years until the advent of Nicolas Copernicus's theory that the sun was the center of the universe. Copernicus was fortunate to live in the late fifteenth and early sixteenth centuries, when man was questioning his place in the universe. Then, a revolution in thinking that would be termed the Renaissance by later generations was taking place. It was not for the fainthearted, for it was dangerous to question religious fate and the creation theory of man's and the universe's existence.

Copernicus was not the first to suggest a heliocentric, or sun-centered, theory of the universe, but his is the most widely known. Born and raised in Poland but doing most of his work in the German states, Copernicus trained as a mathematician and brought his considerable analytical skills to the field of astronomy. In his time, before the invention of powerful telescopes in the early seventeenth century, the known planets were Mercury, Venus, Earth, Mars, Jupiter, and Saturn. Copernicus had trouble accepting the fact that Earth was the center of everything since his observations showed that Mercury at times disappeared in the glare of the sun, suggesting it had a short orbital period around the sun, not Earth. In addition, Mars seemed to be ahead of Earth at one point and then behind Earth, suggesting Earth was also revolving around a larger body at a closer distance than Mars and thus with a faster revolution.

Copernicus, fearful of a religious backlash, kept most of his observations between himself and his assistants. They begged him to publish his work before his death, and he finally relented when he fell ill in 1543. Legend has it that he awoke from a coma and his assistants showed him the finished book of his astronomical theories before he died. Even facing death, he feared the religious authorities and dedicated the book to the pope. Copernicus's work took the scientific community by storm and was more valid than Ptolemy's work, as it had more scientific, especially mathematical, evidence to support his claims. He made one mistake in placing the orbits of the planets in perfect circles, and this would not be corrected until the work of Johannes Kepler in the early seventeenth century proved them to be elliptical in shape.

The motion of the planets and their relation to the sun was also something Copernicus was not entirely correct about either since the theory of gravity was unknown in his time. The work of Isaac Newton may be said to have completed the work started by Copernicus and enhanced by Kepler. The development of the telescope by Galileo and his observations of the planets were further proof of Copernicus's theories. It has even been suggested that the publication of Copernicus's work inflamed the minds of Europe's greatest scientists and was the beginning of the path that led to Kepler, Newton, and Galileo. If so, then Copernicus's one great legacy was the beginning of a scientific revolution that has continued to this day.

Glossary
credence: acceptance of something as being factual

The Structure of the Universe

1 → Humans have questioned the creation of the universe since ancient times and have wondered where and how it came into being and what man's location in it was. Religion and science have often clashed in this search with many people willing to believe that a higher being moves the heavens and Earth while others have looked for a physical explanation. In the past, there were many theories as to Earth's position in this universe; the works of Ptolemy and Nicolas Copernicus were the best known. Their theories differed on a very important point: whether Earth or the sun was the center of the universe. Copernicus's theory, enhanced by the works of other famous scientists, is accepted as fact today.

11 According to paragraph 1, when it came to theories on the creation of the universe, religion and science

Ⓐ agreed in principle on most things
Ⓑ had no relationship with each other
Ⓒ differed somewhat on their teachings
Ⓓ conflicted with each other greatly

2 → Ptolemy's theory suggested that Earth was the center of the universe and that everything revolved around it. Most of his theory was accepted on faith rather than on scientific proof, especially astronomical and mathematical proof. That Earth should be the center of the known realm of mankind did not clash with religious values, seemed natural, and gave **credence** to the idea that man was master of the universe. This theory was held as evident truth for more than one thousand years until the advent of Nicolas Copernicus's theory that the sun was the center of the universe. Copernicus was fortunate to live in the late fifteenth and early sixteenth centuries, when man was questioning his place in the universe. Then, a revolution in thinking that would be termed the Renaissance by later generations was taking place. It was not for the fainthearted, for it was dangerous to question religious fate and the creation theory of man's and the universe's existence.

12 In paragraph 2, the author mentions "the Renaissance" in order to

Ⓐ show that religion was being challenged by ideas

Ⓑ illustrate why Copernicus feared the idea of religion

Ⓒ demonstrate why Copernicus studied astronomy

Ⓓ explain why Copernicus's ideas were accepted

13 In paragraph 2, the author's description of Ptolemy's theory of an Earth-centered universe mentions all of the following EXCEPT:

Ⓐ It was scientifically proven by mathematics.

Ⓑ It seemed to be apparent to everyone.

Ⓒ It agreed with man's opinion of himself.

Ⓓ It did not disagree with religious ideology.

📖 **Glossary**
credence: acceptance of something as being factual

³ ➔ Copernicus was not the first to suggest a heliocentric, or sun-centered, theory of the universe, but his is the most widely known. Born and raised in Poland but doing most of his work in the German states, Copernicus trained as a mathematician and brought his considerable analytical skills to the field of astronomy. In his time, before the invention of powerful telescopes in the early seventeenth century, the known planets were Mercury, Venus, Earth, Mars, Jupiter, and Saturn. Copernicus had trouble accepting the fact that Earth was the center of everything since his observations showed that Mercury at times disappeared in the glare of the sun, suggesting it had a short orbital period around the sun, not Earth. In addition, Mars seemed to be ahead of Earth at one point and then behind Earth, suggesting Earth was also revolving around a larger body at a closer distance than Mars and thus with a faster revolution.

14 The word "considerable" in the passage is closest in meaning to
- Ⓐ noteworthy
- Ⓑ substantial
- Ⓒ appreciative
- Ⓓ attentive

15 According to paragraph 3, which of the following is NOT true of Copernicus?
- Ⓐ He lived in both Poland and some German states.
- Ⓑ His theories were published during his lifetime.
- Ⓒ His education was originally in mathematics.
- Ⓓ He originated the idea of the heliocentric universe.

4 → Copernicus, fearful of a religious backlash, kept most of his observations between himself and his assistants. They begged him to publish his work before his death, and he finally relented when he fell ill in 1543. Legend has it that he awoke from a coma and his assistants showed him the finished book of his astronomical theories before he died. Even facing death, he feared the religious authorities and dedicated the book to the pope. Copernicus's work took the scientific community by storm and was more valid than Ptolemy's work, as it had more scientific, especially mathematical, evidence to support his claims. He made one mistake in placing the orbits of the planets in perfect circles, and this would not be corrected until the work of Johannes Kepler in the early seventeenth century proved them to be elliptical in shape.

16 According to paragraph 4, Copernicus did not publish his theories until near death because he

Ⓐ wanted to make them perfect
Ⓑ thought they were incomplete
Ⓒ feared possible repercussions
Ⓓ wanted to please the pope

5 → The motion of the planets and their relation to the sun was also something Copernicus was not entirely correct about either since the theory of gravity was unknown in his time. The work of Isaac Newton may be said to have completed the work started by Copernicus and enhanced by Kepler. The development of the telescope by Galileo and his observations of the planets were further proof of Copernicus's theories. It has even been suggested that the publication of Copernicus's work inflamed the minds of Europe's greatest scientists and was the beginning of the path that led to Kepler, Newton, and Galileo. If so, then Copernicus's one great legacy was the beginning of a scientific revolution that has continued to this day.

17 Which of the sentences below best expresses the essential information in the highlighted sentence in the passage? *Incorrect* answer choices change the meaning in important ways or leave out essential information.

   A Copernicus knew about gravity but did not think it was related to planetary motion.
   B Copernicus did not understand gravity, so he made some mistakes in his theory.
   C The planets' motions were not correct because gravity did not exist in Copernicus's time.
   D Motion and gravity were related, so Copernicus's theory was incomplete.

18 It can be inferred from paragraph 5 that Galileo, Kepler, and Newton

   A personally met Copernicus
   B read Copernicus's famous work
   C did experiments like Copernicus had done
   D critiqued Copernicus's theories

The motion of the planets and their relation to the sun was also something Copernicus was not entirely correct about either since the theory of gravity was unknown in his time. The work of Isaac Newton may be said to have completed the work started by Copernicus and enhanced by Kepler. ■ The development of the telescope by Galileo and his observations of the planets were further proof of Copernicus's theories. ■ It has even been suggested that the publication of Copernicus's work inflamed the minds of Europe's greatest scientists and was the beginning of the path that led to Kepler, Newton, and Galileo. ■ If so, then Copernicus's one great legacy was the beginning of a scientific revolution that has continued to this day. ■

19 Look at the four squares [■] that indicate where the following sentence could be added to the passage.

However, because of his support of Copernicus's theory, Galileo was hauled before a religious tribunal and forced to recant his belief in the Copernican model of the universe.

Where would the sentence best fit?

Click on a square [■] to add the sentence to the passage.

20 Directions: An introductory sentence for a brief summary of the passage is provided below. Complete the summary by selecting the THREE answer choices that express the most important ideas of the passage. Some sentences do not belong because they express ideas that are not presented in the passage or are minor ideas in the passage. **This question is worth 2 points.**

Drag your answer choices to the spaces where they belong.
To remove an answer choice, click on it. To review the passage, click on **View Text**.

There have been many theories on Earth's position in the universe over time.

-
-
-

Answer Choices

1. Copernicus did not publish his ideas until he was about ready to die.

2. Galileo used his telescope to observe the movement of Jupiter's moons, which helped support Copernicus's theory.

3. Copernicus believed in a theory stating that the sun is the center of the universe and that Earth orbits it.

4. People wanted to believe Earth was the center of the universe because it agreed with their religious views.

5. Kepler and Newton made improvements on the theory proposed by Copernicus.

6. Ptolemy believed that Earth was the center of the universe and that everything else orbited it.

How to Master Skills for the TOEFL® iBT

Actual Test
READING 2

06

TOEFL READING

Reading Section Directions

This section measures your ability to understand academic passages in English. You will have **35 minutes** to read and answer questions about **2 passages**. A clock at the top of the screen will show you how much time is remaining.

Most questions are worth 1 point but the last question for each passage is worth more than 1 point. The directions for the last question indicate how many points you may receive.

Some passages include a word or phrase that is **underlined** in blue. Click on the word or phrase to see a definition or an explanation.

When you want to move to the next question, click on **Next**. You may skip questions and go back to them later. If you want to return to previous questions, click on **Back**. You can click on **Review** at any time, and the review screen will show you which questions you have answered and which you have not answered. From this review screen, you may go directly to any question you have already seen in the Reading section.

Click on **Continue** to go on.

The Cotton Gin

Enslaved people working with a cotton gin

   The United States suddenly found itself the center of world cotton production mainly due to the invention of the cotton gin by Eli Whitney in 1794. The gifted inventor recognized a need to produce cotton more quickly and devised a simple machine to solve that need. Cotton bulbs were cranked through teethed cylinders to remove the stubborn seeds lodged inside the fibrous cotton flowers. Previously, they had to be removed individually by hand, which was a slow, tedious process. Whitney's creation ultimately brought about major social and economic changes in the United States, but it did not result in so many personal changes. Due to legal issues and the overall simplicity of the machine, Whitney himself was never able truly to profit from his groundbreaking invention. Still, the cotton gin changed the face of the United States itself forever, and even today it has evolved into a complex machine which still relies on the basic functions set forth by Whitney.

   The main reason for Whitney's invention was the nature of cotton itself in the mid-Atlantic and southern states. At the time, there were two basic varieties of cotton: long staple and short staple cotton. Long staple cotton thrived in the coastal regions mainly due to the nutrient-rich soil and the fact that its seeds were easily extracted from the cotton fibers; however, land was limited on the coast, and the need to expand inland became vital to furthering the cotton crop industry. Plantation owners quickly discovered that only the short staple variety of cotton could thrive inland, and while it was easily grown, short staple cotton provided a new complication: its sticky seeds. The seeds of short staple cotton literally had to be combed from the cotton fiber by hand before the fiber could be used for textiles. Whitney's invention eliminated this painstaking stage of cotton production and paved the way for cotton to become the new top export of the United States.

   With the advent of the cotton gin, cotton quickly replaced tobacco as the United States' number-one export. With cotton booming, cotton also became the number-one textile in the United States in the early nineteenth century. From the beginning of the century, the cotton yield doubled each proceeding decade up until the Civil War. Virtually overnight, the United States became the leading cotton producer in the entire world, accounting for over seventy-five percent of its production in the southern states. Because of its profitability, more and more land was **razed** with complete disregard for other natural resources, such as forests, to accommodate cotton plantations. Eli Whitney's simple machine, the cotton gin, had ignited social and economic change the young country had never before witnessed. However, it did not necessarily bring only positive change and profit to the South.

While the cotton gin did revolutionize cotton production by removing the seeds easily and making it more efficient, the cotton bulbs themselves still had to be handpicked from the cotton plants. This led to a spike in the need for field workers, which plantation owners filled with more and more slaves. More than the tobacco and sugar crops grown before it, cotton, by virtue of Whitney's cotton gin, contributed to the increase in slavery in the United States. For example, at the end of the eighteenth century, six slave states existed in the United States, yet by the middle of the nineteenth century, at the peak of cotton production, that number had more than doubled to fifteen. While plantation owners reaped the rewards of the cotton boom, slaves suffered brutal, harsh lives in the cotton fields.

Clearly, Whitney could not have predicted the multifaceted influence the cotton gin would have on the United States. He also could not have predicted how little he himself would benefit from it even after it revolutionized the cotton industry. Because of the loose patent laws of the time as well as its simple design, the cotton gin was easily and legally replicated by others. This replication also added to the explosion of cotton on the American and world scene. In turn, slavery reached epic proportions, spreading throughout the South in order to keep the prickly cylinders of the pioneering machine, the cotton gin, spinning.

Glossary
razed: destroyed completely

The Cotton Gin

1 → The United States suddenly found itself the center of world cotton production mainly due to the invention of the cotton gin by Eli Whitney in 1794. The gifted inventor recognized a need to produce cotton more quickly and devised a simple machine to solve that need. Cotton bulbs were cranked through teethed cylinders to remove the stubborn seeds lodged inside the fibrous cotton flowers. Previously, they had to be removed individually by hand, which was a slow, tedious process. Whitney's creation ultimately brought about major social and economic changes in the United States, but it did not result in so many personal changes. Due to legal issues and the overall simplicity of the machine, Whitney himself was never able truly to profit from his groundbreaking invention. Still, the cotton gin changed the face of the United States itself forever, and even today it has evolved into a complex machine which still relies on the basic functions set forth by Whitney.

1. According to paragraph 1, which of the following is true of the cotton gin?
    - Ⓐ It made the American colonies a major cotton producer.
    - Ⓑ Whitney developed it to help crops yield more cotton.
    - Ⓒ It was a basic device which deseeded the cotton.
    - Ⓓ It made Eli Whitney an extremely wealthy man.

2 → The main reason for Whitney's invention was the nature of cotton itself in the mid-Atlantic and southern states. At the time, there were two basic varieties of cotton: long staple and short staple cotton. Long staple cotton thrived in the coastal regions mainly due to the nutrient-rich soil and the fact that its seeds were easily extracted from the cotton fibers; however, land was limited on the coast, and the need to expand inland became vital to furthering the cotton crop industry. Plantation owners quickly discovered that only the short staple variety of cotton could thrive inland, and while it was easily grown, short staple cotton provided a new complication: its sticky seeds. The seeds of short staple cotton literally had to be combed from the cotton fiber by hand before the fiber could be used for textiles. Whitney's invention eliminated this painstaking stage of cotton production and paved the way for cotton to become the new top export of the United States.

2. The author discusses "two basic varieties of cotton" in paragraph 2 in order to
   A) show that long staple cotton was more valuable
   B) contrast the ease of working with both kinds of cotton
   C) note that short staple cotton did not require rich soil
   D) indicate an agricultural error made by plantation owners

3. Which of the sentences below best expresses the essential information in the highlighted sentence in the passage? *Incorrect* answer choices change the meaning in important ways or leave out essential information.
   A) While long staple cotton was grown near the coast for a couple of reasons, farmers needed to farm on land further from the coast in order to produce more cotton.
   B) Although long staple cotton grew well in nutrient-rich soil like that near the coast, farmers could not grow it when they moved inland, so they grew short staple cotton instead.
   C) Because of a lack of land near the coast, long staple cotton was not grown everywhere in the South, which was unfortunate because it had several advantages.
   D) In order to grow more cotton, people began to move inland away from the coast, where long staple cotton could grow more effectively than any other kind of cotton.

2 → The main reason for Whitney's invention was the nature of cotton itself in the mid-Atlantic and southern states. At the time, there were two basic varieties of cotton: long staple and short staple cotton. Long staple cotton thrived in the coastal regions mainly due to the nutrient-rich soil and the fact that its seeds were easily extracted from the cotton fibers; however, land was limited on the coast, and the need to expand inland became vital to furthering the cotton crop industry. Plantation owners quickly discovered that only the short staple variety of cotton could thrive inland, and while it was easily grown, short staple cotton provided a new complication: its sticky seeds. The seeds of short staple cotton literally had to be combed from the cotton fiber by hand before the fiber could be used for textiles. Whitney's invention eliminated this painstaking stage of cotton production and paved the way for cotton to become the new top export of the United States.

4. Which of the following can be inferred from paragraph 2 about long staple cotton?

   Ⓐ It had a greater yield than short staple cotton crops.
   Ⓑ It could not prosper away from the coastal region.
   Ⓒ It had larger seeds which could be accessed easily.
   Ⓓ It depended on sea breezes in order to proliferate.

3 → With the advent of the cotton gin, cotton quickly replaced tobacco as the United States' number-one export. With cotton booming, cotton also became the number-one textile in the United States in the early nineteenth century. From the beginning of the century, the cotton yield doubled each proceeding decade up until the Civil War. Virtually overnight, the United States became the leading cotton producer in the entire world, accounting for over seventy-five percent of its production in the southern states. Because of its profitability, more and more land was **razed** with complete disregard for other natural resources, such as forests, to accommodate cotton plantations. Eli Whitney's simple machine, the cotton gin, had ignited social and economic change the young country had never before witnessed. However, it did not necessarily bring only positive change and profit to the South.

5. Which of the following can be inferred from paragraph 3 about cotton production?

   Ⓐ Cotton could never replace tobacco as the major American cash crop.
   Ⓑ Thirty-five percent of all cotton came from the Americas.
   Ⓒ The value of cotton was placed ahead of that of timber.
   Ⓓ The economic change cotton created could not rival the social one.

Glossary
razed: destroyed completely

⁴→ While the cotton gin did revolutionize cotton production by removing the seeds easily and making it more efficient, the cotton bulbs themselves still had to be handpicked from the cotton plants. This led to a spike in the need for field workers, which plantation owners filled with more and more slaves. More than the tobacco and sugar crops grown before it, cotton, by virtue of Whitney's cotton gin, contributed to the increase in slavery in the United States. For example, at the end of the eighteenth century, six slave states existed in the United States, yet by the middle of the nineteenth century, at the peak of cotton production, that number had more than doubled to fifteen. While plantation owners reaped the rewards of the cotton boom, slaves suffered brutal, harsh lives in the cotton fields.

6. According to paragraph 4, an increase in slaves occurred because

   Ⓐ the cotton gin was not as fast or as efficient as manpower
   Ⓑ plantation owners needed more workers to run their cotton gins
   Ⓒ farmers needed more laborers to pick the cotton from the stems
   Ⓓ more and more states legalized slavery than had previously

5 → Clearly, Whitney could not have predicted the multifaceted influence the cotton gin would have on the United States. He also could not have predicted how little he himself would benefit from it even after it revolutionized the cotton industry. Because of the loose patent laws of the time as well as its simple design, the cotton gin was easily and legally replicated by others. This replication also added to the explosion of cotton on the American and world scene. In turn, slavery reached epic proportions, spreading throughout the South in order to keep the prickly cylinders of the pioneering machine, the cotton gin, spinning.

7. The word "multifaceted" in the passage is closest in meaning to
   A. major
   B. increased
   C. versatile
   D. surprising

8. According to paragraph 5, Whitney did not benefit financially from the cotton gin because
   A. other inventors had already patented the same idea
   B. it was easily mimicked for free by other individuals
   C. better designs replaced it due to their increased efficiency
   D. while he was a talented inventor, he was a poor businessman

While the cotton gin did revolutionize cotton production by removing the seeds easily and making it more efficient, the cotton bulbs themselves still had to be handpicked from the cotton plants. This led to a spike in the need for field workers, which plantation owners filled with more and more slaves. ■ More than the tobacco and sugar crops grown before it, cotton, by virtue of Whitney's cotton gin, contributed to the increase in slavery in the United States. ■ For example, at the end of the eighteenth century, six slave states existed in the United States, yet by the middle of the nineteenth century, at the peak of cotton production, that number had more than doubled to fifteen. ■ While plantation owners reaped the rewards of the cotton boom, slaves suffered brutal, harsh lives in the cotton fields. ■

9. Look at the four squares [■] that indicate where the following sentence could be added to the passage.

Undoubtedly, it had an indirect effect on the slavery environment of the time.

Where would the sentence best fit?

Click on a square [■] to add the sentence to the passage.

Directions: An introductory sentence for a brief summary of the passage is provided below. Complete the summary by selecting the THREE answer choices that express the most important ideas of the passage. Some sentences do not belong because they express ideas that are not presented in the passage or are minor ideas in the passage. **This question is worth 2 points.**

Drag your answer choices to the spaces where they belong.
To remove an answer choice, click on it. To review the passage, click on **View Text**.

Eli Whitney's cotton gin had positive economic effects on the United States as well as socially disastrous ones.

-
-
-

Answer Choices

1. Sugar and tobacco dominated agriculture before cotton.
2. The cotton gin was copied by overzealous enterprisers.
3. The U.S. quickly became a world leader in cotton production.
4. The cotton gin overcame difficulties with short staple cotton.
5. Long staple cotton was replaced with the more resilient short staple version.
6. A drastic increase in the number of slave states occurred.

Musical Benefits

Music surrounds people to such an extent that they frequently take it for granted. It is on computers, TVs, and radios, in people's heads as they hum tunes, in department stores where people shop, and even in elevators. People recognize good and bad music and know when it makes them feel relaxed or excited. Even babies have an uncanny ability to recognize music and know when it is out of tune or a false note is played. Some behavior specialists believe that by studying the relationship between music and physical and psychological benefits, they can uncover the mystery of where music comes from and how it influences man's very survival.

The questions that beg to be answered are why music was developed in the first place and what purpose it has for humans. Perhaps man adapted it from sounds in his environment, from birds and other animals, or from natural sounds such as the sound of using a stone to chip away at an animal bone. There is evidence that music in the form of singing may have begun over 200,000 years ago. The oldest extant instrument, a flute made from bone, is more than 40,000 years old. Mothers from time immemorial have sung their babies to sleep, and it is this relationship between mothers and infants that attracts a lot of study. Babies can recognize musical patterns, and when a false note is played, they will recognize that something is wrong. This suggests that music is not so much learned as imprinted in people's brains while in the womb. Music also seems to have the same universal rhythms that babies understand no matter what culture they come from. This is unlike different languages, which go unrecognized by infants and adults alike because they have no natural imprinting for languages.

The need for music as a part of human survival is what is at the center of an academic debate. Some studies suggest that music is necessary for procreation and use as an example the great number of male musicians in popular culture who attract multiple female companions and produce numerous progeny. Others scoff at this notion by claiming it is an anomaly of the times and historically has no precedent. A further study claims that music actually calms males by making them less sexually aggressive. Using physical evidence from studies of **testosterone** levels in males and females after prolonged listening to music, the study discovered that males had lower testosterone levels and decreased sex drives while women had increased levels and were more assertive and aggressive and thus less attractive to males. This suggests that music had the opposite effect of reducing sexual tension in groups so that chaos would not result from competition over female companions.

The theory of music as a healer has more powerful evidence. Babies lulled to sleep by music sleep longer and more deeply and, as a consequence, are healthier. Music also alleviates stress by reducing the secretion of the hormone cortisol from the adrenal gland. Actually making music rather than listening to it is also beneficial and can release certain immune cells in the body that are used to fight viruses and even cancer cells. Music also reduces fear and tension and makes people seem more a part of a group, as anyone who has attended a live concert can attest. In some societies, music was used to bolster the morale of its soldiers before battle and to make them seem part of a group effort.

Whether humans are born with the ability to understand music or have to learn it is not yet fully understood. Even so, music's ability to revive the human spirit, to reduce stress, and to make people feel a part of a group sets it apart from other arts. Music is even part of modern technological wonders such as motion pictures, television shows, and commercial advertising. The theme song of a favorite show or the soundtrack of a beloved movie can bring a smile to a face or a tear to an eye, but it undoubtedly touches the human spirit in some fascinating way whether ingrained in the human psyche or not.

Glossary
testosterone: a hormone in the human body that appears more commonly in males

Musical Benefits

1 → Music surrounds people to such an extent that they frequently take it for granted. It is on computers, TVs, and radios, in people's heads as they hum tunes, in department stores where people shop, and even in elevators. People recognize good and bad music and know when it makes them feel relaxed or excited. Even babies have an uncanny ability to recognize music and know when it is out of tune or a false note is played. Some behavior specialists believe that by studying the relationship between music and physical and psychological benefits, they can uncover the mystery of where music comes from and how it influences man's very survival.

11. According to paragraph 1, babies have the ability to
   - Ⓐ distinguish the sounds of different musical instruments
   - Ⓑ know when music is correctly played or not
   - Ⓒ understand where different music comes from
   - Ⓓ know music when they are first born

2 → The questions that beg to be answered are why music was developed in the first place and what purpose it has for humans. Perhaps man adapted it from sounds in his environment, from birds and other animals, or from natural sounds such as the sound of using a stone to chip away at an animal bone. There is evidence that music in the form of singing may have begun over 200,000 years ago. The oldest extant instrument, a flute made from bone, is more than 40,000 years old. Mothers from time immemorial have sung their babies to sleep, and it is this relationship between mothers and infants that attracts a lot of study. Babies can recognize musical patterns, and when a false note is played, they will recognize that something is wrong. This suggests that music is not so much learned as imprinted in people's brains while in the womb. Music also seems to have the same universal rhythms that babies understand no matter what culture they come from. This is unlike different languages, which go unrecognized by infants and adults alike because they have no natural imprinting for languages.

12 In paragraph 2, the author's description of possible origins of music mentions all of the following EXCEPT:

Ⓐ The making of the first musical instruments

Ⓑ Humans repeating sounds they made while working

Ⓒ A mother's instinctive caring for her new baby

Ⓓ Humans mimicking animals they heard in the wild

3 → The need for music as a part of human survival is what is at the center of an academic debate. Some studies suggest that music is necessary for procreation and use as an example the great number of male musicians in popular culture who attract multiple female companions and produce numerous progeny. Others scoff at this notion by claiming it is an anomaly of the times and historically has no precedent. A further study claims that music actually calms males by making them less sexually aggressive. Using physical evidence from studies of **testosterone** levels in males and females after prolonged listening to music, the study discovered that males had lower testosterone levels and decreased sex drives while women had increased levels and were more assertive and aggressive and thus less attractive to males. This suggests that music had the opposite effect of reducing sexual tension in groups so that chaos would not result from competition over female companions.

13 Which of the sentences below best expresses the essential information in the highlighted sentence in the passage? *Incorrect* answer choices change the meaning in important ways or leave out essential information.

- Ⓐ Because people cannot reproduce without music, many male pop musicians have more children than people in other professions.
- Ⓑ Studies indicate that male musicians have lots of babies with many different women, thereby proving that they rely on music to do so.
- Ⓒ Because many male pop musicians have large numbers of babies, some researchers believe that music is needed in order to reproduce.
- Ⓓ The biggest example of the importance of music to reproduction is the fact that musicians are more fertile than most other people.

14 According to paragraph 3, prolonged exposure to music makes

- Ⓐ males more sexually aggressive and females more docile
- Ⓑ females and males both less sexually aggressive
- Ⓒ males less sexually aggressive and females more assertive
- Ⓓ females more sexually aggressive and males more assertive

📖 Glossary
testosterone: a hormone in the human body that appears more commonly in males

4 → The theory of music as a healer has more powerful evidence. Babies lulled to sleep by music sleep longer and more deeply and, as a consequence, are healthier. Music also alleviates stress by reducing the secretion of the hormone cortisol from the adrenal gland. Actually making music rather than listening to it is also beneficial and can release certain immune cells in the body that are used to fight viruses and even cancer cells. Music also reduces fear and tension and makes people seem more a part of a group, as anyone who has attended a live concert can attest. In some societies, music was used to bolster the morale of its soldiers before battle and to make them seem part of a group effort.

5 → Whether humans are born with the ability to understand music or have to learn it is not yet fully understood. Even so, music's ability to revive the human spirit, to reduce stress, and to make people feel a part of a group sets it apart from other arts. Music is even part of modern technological wonders such as motion pictures, television shows, and commercial advertising. The theme song of a favorite show or the soundtrack of a beloved movie can bring a smile to a face or a tear to an eye, but it undoubtedly touches the human spirit in some fascinating way whether ingrained in the human psyche or not.

15 The word "it" in the passage refers to
- Ⓐ the secretion
- Ⓑ the hormone cortisol
- Ⓒ the adrenal gland
- Ⓓ music

16 It can be inferred from paragraph 4 that cortisol
- Ⓐ causes increased stress levels
- Ⓑ does nothing to induce stress
- Ⓒ is secreted when music is heard
- Ⓓ is entirely to blame for stress

17 The word "revive" in the passage is closest in meaning to
- Ⓐ enliven
- Ⓑ improve
- Ⓒ restrain
- Ⓓ elevate

18 According to paragraph 5, it is generally accepted that music
- Ⓐ is ingrained from birth
- Ⓑ must be learned after birth
- Ⓒ both heals and spiritualizes
- Ⓓ is everywhere in society

The questions that beg to be answered are why music was developed in the first place and what purpose it has for humans. Perhaps man adapted it from sounds in his environment, from birds and other animals, or from natural sounds such as the sound of using a stone to chip away at an animal bone. There is evidence that music in the form of singing may have begun over 200,000 years ago. The oldest extant instrument, a flute made from bone, is more than 40,000 years old. Mothers from time immemorial have sung their babies to sleep, and it is this relationship between mothers and infants that attracts a lot of study. Babies can recognize musical patterns, and when a false note is played, they will recognize that something is wrong. ■ This suggests that music is not so much learned as imprinted in people's brains while in the womb. ■ Music also seems to have the same universal rhythms that babies understand no matter what culture they come from. ■ This is unlike different languages, which go unrecognized by infants and adults alike because they have no natural imprinting for languages. ■

19 Look at the four squares [■] that indicate where the following sentence could be added to the passage.

In fact, many studies recommend playing music for babies before they are born and also as a part of their early education.

Where would the sentence best fit?

Click on a square [■] to add the sentence to the passage.

20 Directions: An introductory sentence for a brief summary of the passage is provided below. Complete the summary by selecting the THREE answer choices that express the most important ideas of the passage. Some sentences do not belong because they express ideas that are not presented in the passage or are minor ideas in the passage. **This question is worth 2 points.**

Drag your answer choices to the spaces where they belong.
To remove an answer choice, click on it. To review the passage, click on **View Text**.

Academics disagree on the origins of music and its purpose, but it appears to have the power to heal and unify people.

-
-
-

Answer Choices

1. Music seems to have no relationship to the procreation of human life and may have been used to prevent chaos.

2. The ability to distinguish between correct and incorrect rhythms in babies suggests an ingrained musical ability.

3. Archaeological evidence points to the first musical instruments being produced more than 40,000 years ago.

4. Humans have the ability to recognize rhythmic patterns from unfamiliar cultures and musical styles.

5. People engaged in playing musical instruments have reduced levels of hormones that cause stress and increased levels of cancer-fighting immune cells.

6. Mothers have used their singing voices to calm babies and to make them fall asleep since almost the beginning of human existence.

Actual Test

READING 2

07

TOEFL READING

Reading Section Directions

This section measures your ability to understand academic passages in English. You will have **35 minutes** to read and answer questions about **2 passages**. A clock at the top of the screen will show you how much time is remaining.

Most questions are worth 1 point but the last question for each passage is worth more than 1 point. The directions for the last question indicate how many points you may receive.

Some passages include a word or phrase that is **underlined** in blue. Click on the word or phrase to see a definition or an explanation.

When you want to move to the next question, click on **Next**. You may skip questions and go back to them later. If you want to return to previous questions, click on **Back**. You can click on **Review** at any time, and the review screen will show you which questions you have answered and which you have not answered. From this review screen, you may go directly to any question you have already seen in the Reading section.

Click on **Continue** to go on.

American Immigration and Migration

Throughout history, pressures of population have resulted in mass migrations of people seeking new lands for sustenance and opportunity. A prime example is the Germanic tribes that were pushed west into the Roman Empire and eventually contributed to its collapse. Other migrations were for religious reasons, military conquest, the lure of riches, and the opportunity to make better lives for themselves, of which there are numerous examples through history. The discovery of the New World in 1492 led to one of the largest migrations of the human population with many going to the lands that became the United States, the country with the largest population in the Western Hemisphere.

America offered many things to attract these early settlers and those that came after. Many religious sects came in the seventeenth century, a time of religious persecution in Europe, which is why religious toleration was and still is a cornerstone of American policy. The vast and empty land of America was another attraction to Europeans, whose land had been owned and divided by nobles for many centuries. In Europe, a man was either a lord or a peasant who worked the lord's land. America also had fewer class distinctions than most other countries, meaning that no matter what circumstances one was born into, a person could become anything he wanted. This remains one of the greatest attractions of America for modern-day immigrants.

By the time of the American Revolution in 1775, the land had approximately three million people. While the United States as a nation was created from the revolution, it was the nineteenth century that saw the unprecedented expansion of the United States west to the Mississippi River and beyond to the Pacific coast to create the nation it is today. The Louisiana Purchase of 1803 and the Mexican War of 1846-48 dramatically increased the country's size and expanded the nation from the Mississippi to the Pacific Ocean. All of the lands in the west were open for migration but were difficult to get to, with great distances to traverse, hostile Native Americans to deal with, and the harshness of the terrain to contend with. The lands of California and Oregon beckoned with their cool valleys and green pastures, but by the 1840s, few settlers had managed the several-month-long dangerous journey.

This, however, changed in the mid-nineteenth century. Three great events—the discovery of gold in California, the passing of new government legislature, and the opening of the transcontinental railway—changed the pattern of migration. The news of the California gold fields first found in 1848 swept eastward and around the world, attracting thousands upon thousands of adventurers to the west. Still, the lands between the Mississippi and the Rocky Mountains were largely empty. Although during the Civil War of 1861 to 1865, western migration was largely interrupted, in the middle of the war, the government passed one of its great pieces of legislature. The Homestead Act of 1862 allowed anyone who claimed 160 acres and farmed it or lived on it for five years to keep it. Ease of transportation to the west was still a problem, but the completion of the transcontinental railway in 1869 finally provided an efficient means of transportation to the western lands.

Perhaps the greatest influence was the expansion of the nation's population, with tens of thousands leaving the burgeoning cities of the east for greater opportunities west of the Mississippi River. The nineteenth century saw an unprecedented increase in American immigration, still mostly from Europe, including massive migration from Ireland following the potato famine of that impoverished land in the late 1840s. Other large immigrant groups were Germans, Scandinavians, Poles, and, later, Italians. The Homestead Act was designed in part to increase migration from the eastern cities, which were expanding at rapid rates as immigration increased. Tens of thousands left the crowded cities of the east for the promise of free land and the chance to be their own masters. While the desire for farmland is no longer an incentive for immigration, the expansion of the United States has never really stopped, with thousands arriving every year seeking their dreams and hoping they can be found in the land of opportunity.

American Immigration and Migration

1 → Throughout history, pressures of population have resulted in mass migrations of people seeking new lands for sustenance and opportunity. A prime example is the Germanic tribes that were pushed west into the Roman Empire and eventually contributed to its collapse. Other migrations were for religious reasons, military conquest, the lure of riches, and the opportunity to make better lives for themselves, of which there are numerous examples through history. The discovery of the New World in 1492 led to one of the largest migrations of the human population with many going to the lands that became the United States, the country with the largest population in the Western Hemisphere.

1. According to paragraph 1, the collapse of the Roman Empire
   - (A) was partly because of the migration of Germanic tribes
   - (B) was entirely the result of Germanic tribes attacking Rome
   - (C) was uninfluenced by the movement of Germanic tribes
   - (D) happened before the Germanic tribes moved into Roman lands

2. In paragraph 1, the author's description of reasons for migration mentions all of the following EXCEPT:
   - (A) The desire for new opportunities
   - (B) The conquest of other lands
   - (C) Escaping from slavery
   - (D) Increases in population

2 → America offered many things to attract these early settlers and those that came after. Many religious sects came in the seventeenth century, a time of religious persecution in Europe, which is why religious toleration was and still is a cornerstone of American policy. The vast and empty land of America was another attraction to Europeans, whose land had been owned and divided by nobles for many centuries. In Europe, a man was either a lord or a peasant who worked the lord's land. America also had fewer class distinctions than most other countries, meaning that no matter what circumstances one was born into, a person could become anything he wanted. This remains one of the greatest attractions of America for modern-day immigrants.

3. In paragraph 2, the author mentions the "religious persecution" in seventeenth-century Europe in order to

    A explain why there was great turmoil in Europe at that time
    B give a reason why many Europeans came to America
    C show why America had a policy of religious toleration
    D examine the main reason for immigration to America

4. Which of the sentences below best expresses the essential information in the highlighted sentence in the passage? *Incorrect* answer choices change the meaning in important ways or leave out essential information.

    A Even though Americans cared less about class than people in other places, the circumstances of one's birth often dictated what that person would later become.
    B Since a person's parents were not a barrier to doing something later in life in America, people made more distinctions between the U.S. and other countries.
    C Because Americans were less concerned about class than people in other countries, a person could do anything no matter what his station in birth was.
    D People in America could do anything they desired since the circumstances of their birth affected them there more than they did in other countries.

3 → By the time of the American Revolution in 1775, the land had approximately three million people. While the United States as a nation was created from the revolution, it was the nineteenth century that saw the unprecedented expansion of the United States west to the Mississippi River and beyond to the Pacific coast to create the nation it is today. The Louisiana Purchase of 1803 and the Mexican War of 1846-48 dramatically increased the country's size and expanded the nation from the Mississippi to the Pacific Ocean. All of the lands in the west were open for migration but were difficult to get to, with great distances to traverse, hostile Native Americans to deal with, and the harshness of the terrain to contend with. The lands of California and Oregon beckoned with their cool valleys and green pastures, but by the 1840s, few settlers had managed the several-month-long dangerous journey.

5. It can be inferred from paragraph 3 that during the early westward expansion, few people settled in the lands between the Mississippi River and California because

   Ⓐ difficult environmental circumstances existed
   Ⓑ there was no free land available in this area
   Ⓒ the government wanted them to move west
   Ⓓ the land was not owned by the United States

This, however, changed in the mid-nineteenth century. Three great events—the discovery of gold in California, the passing of new government legislature, and the opening of the transcontinental railway—changed the pattern of migration. The news of the California gold fields first found in 1848 swept eastward and around the world, attracting thousands upon thousands of adventurers to the west. Still, the lands between the Mississippi and the Rocky Mountains were largely empty. Although during the Civil War of 1861 to 1865, western migration was largely interrupted, in the middle of the war, the government passed one of its great pieces of legislature. The Homestead Act of 1862 allowed anyone who claimed 160 acres and farmed it or lived on it for five years to keep it. Ease of transportation to the west was still a problem, but the completion of the transcontinental railway in 1869 finally provided an efficient means of transportation to the western lands.

6 The word "interrupted" in the passage is closest in meaning to

Ⓐ prevented
Ⓑ continued
Ⓒ stopped
Ⓓ interfered

5 ➔ Perhaps the greatest influence was the expansion of the nation's population, with tens of thousands leaving the burgeoning cities of the east for greater opportunities west of the Mississippi River. The nineteenth century saw an unprecedented increase in American immigration, still mostly from Europe, including massive migration from Ireland following the potato famine of that impoverished land in the late 1840s. Other large immigrant groups were Germans, Scandinavians, Poles, and, later, Italians. The Homestead Act was designed in part to increase migration from the eastern cities, which were expanding at rapid rates as immigration increased. Tens of thousands left the crowded cities of the east for the promise of free land and the chance to be their own masters. While the desire for farmland is no longer an incentive for immigration, the expansion of the United States has never really stopped, with thousands arriving every year seeking their dreams and hoping they can be found in the land of opportunity.

7. According to paragraph 5, the Irish immigrated in vast numbers to the United States because of

   Ⓐ a food shortage in Ireland
   Ⓑ a terrible war in Ireland
   Ⓒ the great poverty of their land
   Ⓓ the loss of all their land

8. According to paragraph 5, the Homestead Act was passed by the American government to

   Ⓐ prevent immigrants from coming to the eastern cities
   Ⓑ develop the interior lands of the nation
   Ⓒ give everyone a chance to own land
   Ⓓ encourage migration from cities to the western lands

By the time of the American Revolution in 1775, the land had approximately three million people. While the United States as a nation was created from the revolution, it was the nineteenth century that saw the unprecedented expansion of the United States west to the Mississippi River and beyond to the Pacific coast to create the nation it is today. ■ The Louisiana Purchase of 1803 and the Mexican War of 1846-48 dramatically increased the country's size and expanded the nation from the Mississippi to the Pacific Ocean. ■ All of the lands in the west were open for migration but were difficult to get to, with great distances to traverse, hostile Native Americans to deal with, and the harshness of the terrain to contend with. ■ The lands of California and Oregon beckoned with their cool valleys and green pastures, but by the 1840s, few settlers had managed the several-month-long dangerous journey. ■

9. Look at the four squares [■] that indicate where the following sentence could be added to the passage.

In addition to the vast distance, there were dry, dusty plains, scorching deserts, and treacherous mountains to cross.

Where would the sentence best fit?

Click on a square [■] to add the sentence to the passage.

10 Directions: An introductory sentence for a brief summary of the passage is provided below. Complete the summary by selecting the THREE answer choices that express the most important ideas of the passage. Some sentences do not belong because they express ideas that are not presented in the passage or are minor ideas in the passage. **This question is worth 2 points.**

Drag your answer choices to the spaces where they belong.
To remove an answer choice, click on it. To review the passage, click on **View Text**.

People immigrated to America for various reasons, and many migrated westward for new opportunities.

-
-
-

Answer Choices

1. The United States often acquired new land, so people moved onto this land and settled it.

2. The Louisiana Purchase in 1803 more than doubled the size of the United States.

3. America's population was three million in 1775 but grew much larger in the 1800s and 1900s.

4. In the early years of American immigration, people often came because of religious persecution and land opportunities.

5. In the 1800s, massive immigration from Europe led to people traveling west to seek new chances.

6. The Homestead Act of 1862 gave people some land so long as they would farm it.

The Coral Snake and the Diamondback Rattlesnake

An eastern coral snake

In the United States and other parts of North and South America, there are three main types of venomous snakes as defined by their **genera**: *Agkistrodon*, *Crotalus*, and *Micrurus*. All are potentially dangerous to humans due to their highly toxic venom. More specifically, *Agkistrodon* and *Crotalus* are commonly known as vipers while *Micrurus* is more widely known as elapids. There are many noteworthy differences between these two kinds of venomous snakes. One is the type of fangs each snake employs to attack prey or to defend itself. Another is the way the snake's venom affects its prey. Two of the best examples of the elapid and the viper in the United States are the coral snake and the diamondback rattlesnake, respectively. While both are among the most beautiful in the reptile world, their beauty disguises their potentially fatal effects.

The coral snake is a relative of the king cobra found in Asia. In the Americas, it enjoys the tropical climates of the Southeast. It is diurnal, hunting mainly during the day for smaller reptiles and rodents, and it typically burrows underground. One of its most distinguishing features is its brightly colored red, yellow, and black bands—the pattern that other species of snakes have evolved to mimic as a defense against predators. This is proof of the coral snake's potency and a clear sign to those who might stumble upon one. Only the coral snake has red bands bordered by yellow ones, denoting its authenticity, and though they may look similar to the coral snake, other false coral snakes lack the venom and the fangs of the true one.

The coral snake's venom is twice as potent as that of the diamondback rattlesnake. It contains a neurotoxin that attacks the nervous system of other animals and eventually causes paralysis.

However, the coral snake, unlike true vipers such as the diamondback rattlesnake, has short, small permanent fangs in its upper jaw, which permit the slow secretion of venom. Therefore, the coral snake must grasp and continue to hold on to its prey for its venom to be effective. Vipers, on the other hand, have a pair of retractable, hollow fangs of greater size than the coral snake that can inflict a bite and jet in enough venom to incapacitate their prey in a split second. This is the main reason why the diamondback rattlesnake, not the coral snake, is considered the deadliest snake in the United States: It by far accounts for a higher number of human fatalities each year.

The infamous diamondback rattlesnake contains a more complex set of hunting and attacking devices than the coral snake and other elapids. It is a pit viper, which denotes the small heat sensors on its face used to detect warm-blooded prey such as rodents and birds. The diamondback rattlesnake is primarily nocturnal and has a much larger body size than the coral snake. The diamondback rattlesnake can often reach lengths of up to eight feet while few coral snakes ever attain half that size. Additionally, the rattlesnake's fangs are hollow and occupy the upper jaw against the roof of the mouth until an actual strike, at which time they spring down for action. Moreover, backup sets of fangs replace the ones that remain lodged in prey, much like the replacement system of teeth found in sharks. As regards venom, the diamondback rattlesnake contains a hemotoxin that attacks the blood and the primary organs such as its prey's heart. Unlike the coral snake, the diamondback rattlesnake's venom causes extensive damage to tissues around the bite area as well as excruciating pain.

Ultimately, especially when it comes to human safety, the coral snake is clearly the lesser of two evils. First, because of its colorful bands, it is more easily seen than the rattlesnake, which blends in more with the colors of its habitat. The coral snake broadcasts its presence while the rattlesnake camouflages itself. Second, an initial bite by a coral snake is probably not sufficient to get enough neurotoxins into the human body. This gives an individual time to retreat. In contrast, many attacks by the deadly diamondback rattlesnake occur before it is even seen by the victim, resulting in pain and possibly death.

Glossary
genera: subdivisions of families of animals or plants

The Coral Snake and the Diamondback Rattlesnake

1 → In the United States and other parts of North and South America, there are three main types of venomous snakes as defined by their **genera**: *Agkistrodon*, *Crotalus*, and *Micrurus*. All are potentially dangerous to humans due to their highly toxic venom. More specifically, *Agkistrodon* and *Crotalus* are commonly known as vipers while *Micrurus* is more widely known as elapids. There are many noteworthy differences between these two kinds of venomous snakes. One is the type of fangs each snake employs to attack prey or to defend itself. Another is the way the snake's venom affects its prey. Two of the best examples of the elapid and the viper in the United States are the coral snake and the diamondback rattlesnake, respectively. While both are among the most beautiful in the reptile world, their beauty disguises their potentially fatal effects.

Glossary
genera: subdivisions of families of animals or plants

11 According to paragraph 1, which of the following is true of venomous snakes in the Americas?

Ⓐ All types can prove to be fatal to animals and human beings.
Ⓑ Most display beautiful color configurations on their bodies.
Ⓒ They are differentiated by the types of fangs that they have.
Ⓓ Different kinds use the same type of venom for defense.

2 → The coral snake is a relative of the king cobra found in Asia. In the Americas, it enjoys the tropical climates of the Southeast. It is diurnal, hunting mainly during the day for smaller reptiles and rodents, and it typically burrows underground. One of its most distinguishing features is its brightly colored red, yellow, and black bands—the pattern that other species of snakes have evolved to mimic as a defense against predators. This is proof of the coral snake's potency and a clear sign to those who might stumble upon one. Only the coral snake has red bands bordered by yellow ones, denoting its authenticity, and though they may look similar to the coral snake, other false coral snakes lack the venom and the fangs of the true one.

12 Which of the sentences below best expresses the essential information in the highlighted sentence in the passage? *Incorrect* answer choices change the meaning in important ways or leave out essential information.

Ⓐ True coral snakes have colorful bands and venomous fangs while false ones, despite their possible similarity in appearance, do not have those fangs.

Ⓑ False coral snakes may have red and yellow bands showing their venomous nature while true ones with similar bands have venomous fangs.

Ⓒ It is almost impossible to distinguish between true coral snakes and false ones because they all have red bands fringed with yellow ones on their bodies.

Ⓓ True coral snakes and false ones may look exactly the same in appearance, but the latter cannot attack and kill prey because they do not have fangs.

13 Which of the following can be inferred from paragraph 2 about the coral snake?

Ⓐ There are other species of snakes that look like it.

Ⓑ The coral snake cannot eat very large animals.

Ⓒ Its bright-colored bands are thick rather than thin.

Ⓓ It was imported by traders from Asia a long time ago.

3 → The coral snake's venom is twice as potent as that of the diamondback rattlesnake. It contains a neurotoxin that attacks the nervous system of other animals and eventually causes paralysis. However, the coral snake, unlike true vipers such as the diamondback rattlesnake, has short, small permanent fangs in its upper jaw, which permit the slow secretion of venom. Therefore, the coral snake must grasp and continue to hold on to its prey for its venom to be effective. Vipers, on the other hand, have a pair of retractable, hollow fangs of greater size than the coral snake that can inflict a bite and jet in enough venom to incapacitate their prey in a split second. This is the main reason why the diamondback rattlesnake, not the coral snake, is considered the deadliest snake in the United States: It by far accounts for a higher number of human fatalities each year.

14. The author discusses the coral snake's "fangs" in paragraph 3 in order to
    Ⓐ note that the venom in them is twice as strong as the rattlesnake's
    Ⓑ show how they are much larger than the fangs of a viper
    Ⓒ contrast their use to that of the diamondback rattlesnake's
    Ⓓ mention how they retract into the cavity of the snake's mouth

15. According to paragraph 3, why are diamondback rattlesnakes the deadliest snakes in the United States?
    Ⓐ They use a smaller amount of venom when attacking humans.
    Ⓑ Their venom is twice as potent as that of the coral snake.
    Ⓒ They have larger fangs and can inject their venom quickly.
    Ⓓ They are much more aggressive than the smaller coral snake.

⁴ ➡ The infamous diamondback rattlesnake contains a more complex set of hunting and attacking devices than the coral snake and other elapids. It is a pit viper, which denotes the small heat sensors on its face used to detect warm-blooded prey such as rodents and birds. The diamondback rattlesnake is primarily nocturnal and has a much larger body size than the coral snake. The diamondback rattlesnake can often reach lengths of up to eight feet while few coral snakes ever attain half that size. Additionally, the rattlesnake's fangs are hollow and occupy the upper jaw against the roof of the mouth until an actual strike, at which time they spring down for action. Moreover, backup sets of fangs replace the ones that remain lodged in prey, much like the replacement system of teeth found in sharks. As regards venom, the diamondback rattlesnake contains a hemotoxin that attacks the blood and the primary organs such as its prey's heart. Unlike the coral snake, the diamondback rattlesnake's venom causes extensive damage to tissues around the bite area as well as excruciating pain.

16. Which of the following can be inferred from paragraph 4 about the diamondback rattlesnake's fangs?

Ⓐ They are similar in shape and size to the teeth of sharks.
Ⓑ They are much longer and sharper than the coral snake's.
Ⓒ They are often embedded in an animal during an attack.
Ⓓ They cause a lot of damage to the area of the initial bite.

5 → Ultimately, especially when it comes to human safety, the coral snake is clearly the lesser of two evils. First, because of its colorful bands, it is more easily seen than the rattlesnake, which blends in more with the colors of its habitat. The coral snake broadcasts its presence while the rattlesnake camouflages itself. Second, an initial bite by a coral snake is probably not sufficient to get enough neurotoxins into the human body. This gives an individual time to retreat. In contrast, many attacks by the deadly diamondback rattlesnake occur before it is even seen by the victim, resulting in pain and possibly death.

17 The word "retreat" in the passage is closest in meaning to

Ⓐ move back
Ⓑ get back
Ⓒ fight back
Ⓓ hold back

18 According to paragraph 5, the coral snake is somewhat less dangerous to humans than the diamondback rattlesnake because

Ⓐ the coral snake is able to camouflage itself better in the wild
Ⓑ the coral snake is noticeable enough for prey to avoid
Ⓒ the coral snake does not have enough venom to harm a person
Ⓓ the coral snake has smaller fangs and less deadly venom

The infamous diamondback rattlesnake contains a more complex set of hunting and attacking devices than the coral snake and other elapids. It is a pit viper, which denotes the small heat sensors on its face used to detect warm-blooded prey such as rodents and birds. ■ The diamondback rattlesnake is primarily nocturnal and has a much larger body size than the coral snake. ■ The diamondback rattlesnake can often reach lengths of up to eight feet while few coral snakes ever attain half that size. ■ Additionally, the rattlesnake's fangs are hollow and occupy the upper jaw against the roof of the mouth until an actual strike, at which time they spring down for action. ■ Moreover, backup sets of fangs replace the ones that remain lodged in prey, much like the replacement system of teeth found in sharks. As regards venom, the diamondback rattlesnake contains a hemotoxin that attacks the blood and the primary organs such as its prey's heart. Unlike the coral snake, the diamondback rattlesnake's venom causes extensive damage to tissues around the bite area as well as excruciating pain.

19 Look at the four squares [■] that indicate where the following sentence could be added to the passage.

Furthermore, they help the snake find food fairly easily.

Where would the sentence best fit?

Click on a square [■] to add the sentence to the passage.

20 Directions: An introductory sentence for a brief summary of the passage is provided below. Complete the summary by selecting the THREE answer choices that express the most important ideas of the passage. Some sentences do not belong because they express ideas that are not presented in the passage or are minor ideas in the passage. **This question is worth 2 points.**

Drag your answer choices to the spaces where they belong. To remove an answer choice, click on it. To review the passage, click on **View Text**.

Two types of venomous snakes are the coral snake and the diamondback rattlesnake.

-
-
-

Answer Choices

1. The coral snake is an elapid whereas the diamondback rattlesnake is a type of viper.

2. The coral snake must hold onto its victims while it bites them to inject its venom.

3. The diamondback rattlesnake's bite is not only powerful but is also painful and damages tissue.

4. The brightly colored coral snake has extremely potent venom and is quite dangerous.

5. The diamondback rattlesnake is more dangerous than the coral snake due to coloration and its method of attack.

6. Both of these snakes can be found in different parts of North and South America.

Actual Test

How to Master Skills for the TOEFL® iBT

Actual Test
READING 2

08

TOEFL READING

Reading Section Directions

This section measures your ability to understand academic passages in English. You will have **35 minutes** to read and answer questions about **2 passages**. A clock at the top of the screen will show you how much time is remaining.

Most questions are worth 1 point but the last question for each passage is worth more than 1 point. The directions for the last question indicate how many points you may receive.

Some passages include a word or phrase that is **underlined** in blue. Click on the word or phrase to see a definition or an explanation.

When you want to move to the next question, click on **Next**. You may skip questions and go back to them later. If you want to return to previous questions, click on **Back**. You can click on **Review** at any time, and the review screen will show you which questions you have answered and which you have not answered. From this review screen, you may go directly to any question you have already seen in the Reading section.

Click on **Continue** to go on.

The Rivers of the Amazon

The Amazon Rainforest

There are three different types of rivers associated with the Amazon Rainforest. Of course, these types exist elsewhere in the world, yet in the Amazon, they are the most distinct. They are classified as whitewater, clearwater, and blackwater rivers, and each displays elements that make it ecologically distinct from the others. Clearly, one of the main reasons they have been named as such is due to the qualities of their appearance, but there are also fundamental differences in everything from their water consistency to abundance or lack of organisms within each type of river. While whitewater and blackwater rivers occupy areas on the floor of the forest at minimal elevations, clearwater rivers tend to be present at higher elevations in mountainous regions. Still, each contributes in its own way to one of the most diverse ecosystems on the planet, the Amazon.

The clearwater rivers of the Amazon region, also called bluewater rivers, are noted for their crystal-clear water and are found flowing through the rocks of the highlands and at upper elevations. One of the main reasons why the waters are so clear is that the rocks they flow through and over are extremely old, making erosion by the river waters difficult. This absence of erosion lends to a lack of sediment in the water and its more transparent nature. Clearwater rivers are also much swifter than whitewater or blackwater rivers due to their abrupt changes in gradients. Overall, clearwater rivers have a very high mineral content, which allows plant life as well as algae to proliferate. Because of the abundance of algae, many other types of species of fish are able to thrive as well.

A second major type of river found in the Amazon is the whitewater river. The formidable Amazon River itself is in this class. Ironically, whitewater rivers are usually light-chocolate colored and have extremely low visibility because they contain heavy loads of sediment. Two of the main causes of their high sediment content are the natural erosion of the river basin itself as well as the deforestation of the rainforest. As deforestation continues, soil is no longer anchored by the roots of vegetation and trees and is instead washed into the river during the heavy rains that frequent the rainforest. Still, whitewater rivers are inherently rich in nutrients and therefore support numerous types of aquatic organisms. In contrast to clearwater rivers, whitewater rivers such as the Amazon tend to flow much more slowly because of the low gradients involved. For example, the Amazon itself experiences only a 107-meter change in elevation from Peru to its mouth, a distance that covers more than 3,219 kilometers.

The final major type of river in the Amazon is known as a blackwater river, of which the Rio Negro in Brazil is a prime example and also the largest in the world. Blackwater rivers are the most common type in the Amazon. They exhibit a deep dark brown color due to the decomposition of leaves and vegetation in the waters. Most vegetation contains the chemical tannin, which is released into blackwater rivers as it begins to decompose. Blackwater rivers have excellent water clarity due to their highly acidic nature, which also benefits the river in a couple of other ways. A high acid content is an excellent trait for a river to have because it keeps the river clean and, in many ways, more sanitary than others. The acid kills parasites and bacteria that can threaten fish populations as well as insect larvae such as that of mosquitoes, which reduces the spread of dangerous diseases such as malaria.

While the Amazon is a highly diverse ecosystem, one of the reasons this is so is due to the different types of river systems within it. The Amazon is the main vein, and most blackwater and clearwater rivers are estuaries or branches of it until they finally link at certain points along the Amazon's main route. For example, the Amazon and the Rio Negro finally meet at Manaus, Brazil, and, once they do, their distinct ecosystems combine to form an even more complex river system of life and water quality until it eventually empties into the ocean.

The Rivers of the Amazon

1 → There are three different types of rivers associated with the Amazon Rainforest. Of course, these types exist elsewhere in the world, yet in the Amazon, they are the most distinct. They are classified as whitewater, clearwater, and blackwater rivers, and each displays elements that make it ecologically distinct from the others. Clearly, one of the main reasons they have been named as such is due to the qualities of their appearance, but there are also fundamental differences in everything from their water consistency to abundance or lack of organisms within each type of river. While whitewater and blackwater rivers occupy areas on the floor of the forest at minimal elevations, clearwater rivers tend to be present at higher elevations in mountainous regions. Still, each contributes in its own way to one of the most diverse ecosystems on the planet, the Amazon.

1. According to paragraph 1, which of the following is true of the major types of Amazon rivers?
   - Ⓐ They are classified by what is able to exist in them.
   - Ⓑ They are determined by their length and breadth.
   - Ⓒ They are unique only to the area of the Amazon.
   - Ⓓ They are all located at altitudes at or beneath sea level.

² → The clearwater rivers of the Amazon region, also called bluewater rivers, are noted for their crystal-clear water and are found flowing through the rocks of the highlands and at upper elevations. One of the main reasons why the waters are so clear is that the rocks they flow through and over are extremely old, making erosion by the river waters difficult. This absence of erosion lends to a lack of sediment in the water and its more transparent nature. Clearwater rivers are also much swifter than whitewater or blackwater rivers due to their abrupt changes in gradients. Overall, clearwater rivers have a very high mineral content, which allows plant life as well as algae to proliferate. Because of the abundance of algae, many other types of species of fish are able to thrive as well.

2 The word "transparent" in the passage is closest in meaning to
- Ⓐ veneered
- Ⓑ refreshing
- Ⓒ glassy
- Ⓓ beneficial

3 Which of the following can be inferred from paragraph 2 about clearwater rivers?
- Ⓐ Their water is not really as clear as their name implies.
- Ⓑ They flow at a slower pace than blackwater rivers.
- Ⓒ There is not much algae present in clearwater rivers.
- Ⓓ They do not exist on more level areas in the Amazon.

4 According to paragraph 2, which of the following is NOT true of clearwater rivers?
- Ⓐ They eventually connect with the Amazon River itself.
- Ⓑ They have very high levels of nutrients and minerals.
- Ⓒ They have enough sediment for algae to multiply.
- Ⓓ They often occur where ancient stones or boulders are present.

³ ➔ A second major type of river found in the Amazon is the whitewater river. The formidable Amazon River itself is in this class. Ironically, whitewater rivers are usually light-chocolate colored and have extremely low visibility because they contain heavy loads of sediment. Two of the main causes of their high sediment content are the natural erosion of the river basin itself as well as the deforestation of the rainforest. As deforestation continues, soil is no longer anchored by the roots of vegetation and trees and is instead washed into the river during the heavy rains that frequent the rainforest. Still, whitewater rivers are inherently rich in nutrients and therefore support numerous types of aquatic organisms. In contrast to clearwater rivers, whitewater rivers such as the Amazon tend to flow much more slowly because of the low gradients involved. For example, the Amazon itself experiences only a 107-meter change in elevation from Peru to its mouth, a distance that covers more than 3,219 kilometers.

5 The author discusses "natural erosion" in paragraph 3 in order to

Ⓐ indicate the types of threats the Amazon region faces
Ⓑ relate why whitewater rivers are not as clear as some others
Ⓒ show how deforestation contributes little to whitewater rivers
Ⓓ suggest that sediment is not the main cause of the colors of rivers

6 According to paragraph 3, deforestation is a negative factor in the Amazon because

Ⓐ too many trees are cut down and will never be replaced
Ⓑ valuable soil is washed away into the rivers
Ⓒ other species of animals will not have a natural habitat
Ⓓ rivers become more erosive without strong boundaries

⁴→ The final major type of river in the Amazon is known as a blackwater river, of which the Rio Negro in Brazil is a prime example and also the largest in the world. Blackwater rivers are the most common type in the Amazon. They exhibit a deep dark brown color due to the decomposition of leaves and vegetation in the waters. Most vegetation contains the chemical tannin, which is released into blackwater rivers as it begins to decompose. Blackwater rivers have excellent water clarity due to their highly acidic nature, which also benefits the river in a couple of other ways. A high acid content is an excellent trait for a river to have because it keeps the river clean and, in many ways, more sanitary than others. The acid kills parasites and bacteria that can threaten fish populations as well as insect larvae such as that of mosquitoes, which reduces the spread of dangerous diseases such as malaria.

7. According to paragraph 4, blackwater rivers are named so because

   Ⓐ they lack the necessary nutrients needed to produce life

   Ⓑ they are in direct contrast to the two other types of rivers

   Ⓒ they are colored by the decomposition of vegetation

   Ⓓ they are the most common type of river in the Amazon

While the Amazon is a highly diverse ecosystem, one of the reasons this is so is due to the different types of river systems within it. The Amazon is the main vein, and most blackwater and clearwater rivers are estuaries or branches of it until they finally link at certain points along the Amazon's main route. **For example, the Amazon and the Rio Negro finally meet at Manaus, Brazil, and, once they do, their distinct ecosystems combine to form an even more complex river system of life and water quality until it eventually empties into the ocean.**

8. Which of the sentences below best expresses the essential information in the highlighted sentence in the passage? *Incorrect* answer choices change the meaning in important ways or leave out essential information.

   Ⓐ The meeting of the Amazon and Rio Negro rivers forms the biggest, most complex river that is teeming with life until it finally reaches the ocean.

   Ⓑ Once the Amazon and the Rio Negro combine, their ecosystems become incredibly diverse all the way until the river makes it to the ocean.

   Ⓒ While the Amazon is more complex than the Rio Negro, once the two meet in Brazil, they form a very complex ecosystem that lasts until the Atlantic Ocean.

   Ⓓ From Manaus to the ocean, the Amazon and Rio Negro rivers combine to form an ecosystem the likes of which the world has never witnessed.

There are three different types of rivers associated with the Amazon Rainforest. Of course, these types exist elsewhere in the world, yet in the Amazon, they are the most distinct. ■ They are classified as whitewater, clearwater, and blackwater rivers, and each displays elements that make it ecologically distinct from the others. ■ Clearly, one of the main reasons they have been named as such is due to the qualities of their appearance, but there are also fundamental differences in everything from their water consistency to abundance or lack of organisms within each type of river. ■ While whitewater and blackwater rivers occupy areas on the floor of the forest at minimal elevations, clearwater rivers tend to be present at higher elevations in mountainous regions. ■ Still, each contributes in its own way to one of the most diverse ecosystems on the planet, the Amazon.

9 Look at the four squares [■] that indicate where the following sentence could be added to the passage.

For example, blackwater rivers contain few or no microorganisms.

Where would the sentence best fit?

Click on a square [■] to add the sentence to the passage.

10 Directions: An introductory sentence for a brief summary of the passage is provided below. Complete the summary by selecting the THREE answer choices that express the most important ideas of the passage. Some sentences do not belong because they express ideas that are not presented in the passage or are minor ideas in the passage. **This question is worth 2 points.**

Drag your answer choices to the spaces where they belong.
To remove an answer choice, click on it. To review the passage, click on **View Text**.

The Amazon region has whitewater, bluewater, and blackwater rivers.

-
-
-

Answer Choices

1. Whitewater rivers in the Amazon region have a lot of sediment and flow slowly.

2. There are many different rivers in South America that flow into the Amazon at some point.

3. The bluewater rivers of the Amazon flow at high elevations and are full of clear water.

4. The Rio Negro River meets the Amazon at Manaus, Brazil, and then goes to the ocean.

5. There is only a 107-meter change in elevation in the Amazon from Peru to the Atlantic Ocean.

6. The Amazon region has many blackwater rivers, which are full of decomposing leaves and vegetation.

Literary Naturalism

One of the most pivotal moments in American literature occurred near the end of the nineteenth century as authors such as a young man named Stephen Crane began to embrace a literary style which was forged in Europe a bit earlier and which would come to be known as naturalism. Crane was born to parents in the ministry and grew up in a household grounded in religious beliefs and context. Yet before long, Crane had, for the most part, rejected religion and the idea of divine intervention in favor of a more hands-on approach to the world. As he began to develop as a writer, naturalist themes of man versus nature, the unrelenting power of nature, and an objective view of the world began to dominate his writing. Naturalists attempted to depict the most accurate view of life unadulterated and unobstructed by external commentary or spiritual intervention. Ultimately, Crane's masterful short story *The Open Boat* stands as one of the most complete and developed works of the naturalist genre.

The first apparent element of naturalism in *The Open Boat* is its subject matter—a shipwreck. Being as true to life as possible is one of the most common goals of a naturalistic writer, and in this short story, Crane is no exception. It did not come from Crane's imagination. Rather, it stemmed from his personal experience. As a young war reporter, Crane was on his way from Florida to Cuba when his vessel, the *Commodore*, encountered a violent **tempest**. Within hours, the ship had sunk, leaving a few lucky survivors on a tiny lifeboat to be subjected to the fury of nature. Throughout the story, Crane depicts scene after scene as if they were snapshots or a short film of what the men in the boat were up against. Through his prose, Crane is able to reveal the unadulterated, brutal realism manifest in nature itself.

As Crane continues with the theme of man versus nature in *The Open Boat*, the element of pessimism, crucial to any naturalistic work, becomes quite apparent. The men are at the mercy of the storms and the seas and cannot do much to save themselves. In this sense, Crane reveals the indifference of nature and the universe in relation to the life or plight of human beings in general. It is obvious to him that angels will not swoop down and save the unfortunate men. The situation of the shipwreck is ideal because ordinary everyday people must face an extreme situation from which it is more than likely that they will perish. Crane continually creates a mood of impending doom and the punishing nature of the universe throughout the story. Along the way, he provides little commentary on the situation, forcing readers to place themselves immediately on the boat with the men while enforcing the dark tone of the story. But even to Crane and most naturalist writers, all is not lost.

Though the outcome is bleak, Crane does add a glimmer of hope to the story. While in general, the individuals may seem insignificant in the grand scheme of the universe or to nature itself, Crane instills the importance of camaraderie in the story. In order to survive, the individuals in the boat must cooperate and help one another against the forces of nature. Together, they have some dominion of control over their fate, but less so individually. Though they are isolated out among the waves in sight of shore, they remain unified in their struggle for survival, which undermines the predominant pessimistic outlook of the story as a whole.

While Crane's work *The Open Boat* is a dark account of a chance situation that turns fatal for many, but not all, of the crew of the *Commodore*, it also sets forth the main elements of a naturalistic literary work at the turn of the twentieth century. Despite the fact that nature can be unrelenting and compassionless toward humans at any given moment, Crane ultimately shows how individuals still always have the capacity to strive together to overcome hardships and disaster. Furthermore, the accuracy and detail by Crane shun any possibility of a sugarcoated reality and reveal the true ferocity of nature as it is.

Glossary
tempest: a violent rain and wind storm; a hurricane

Literary Naturalism

¹→ One of the most pivotal moments in American literature occurred near the end of the nineteenth century as authors such as a young man named Stephen Crane began to embrace a literary style which was forged in Europe a bit earlier and which would come to be known as naturalism. Crane was born to parents in the ministry and grew up in a household grounded in religious beliefs and context. Yet before long, Crane had, for the most part, rejected religion and the idea of divine intervention in favor of a more hands-on approach to the world. As he began to develop as a writer, naturalist themes of man versus nature, the unrelenting power of nature, and an objective view of the world began to dominate his writing. Naturalists attempted to depict the most accurate view of life unadulterated and unobstructed by external commentary or spiritual intervention. Ultimately, Crane's masterful short story *The Open Boat* stands as one of the most complete and developed works of the naturalist genre.

11 Which of the sentences below best expresses the essential information in the highlighted sentence in the passage? *Incorrect* answer choices change the meaning in important ways or leave out essential information.

- Ⓐ Naturalists liked to place their own opinions on spirituality in their writing.
- Ⓑ Naturalists placed more emphasis on representing life as it appeared to them.
- Ⓒ Naturalists tried to embody the most precise view of life by looking to religion.
- Ⓓ Naturalists believed that life was obstructed by outside ambition and spirituality.

12 Which of the following can be inferred from paragraph 1 about Stephen Crane?

- Ⓐ He enjoyed the ministry and listening to preachers.
- Ⓑ He did not enjoy writing when he was young.
- Ⓒ He was rivaled by no other author of his time.
- Ⓓ He was not in accord with the beliefs of his parents.

2 ➡ The first apparent element of naturalism in *The Open Boat* is its subject matter—a shipwreck. Being as true to life as possible is one of the most common goals of a naturalistic writer, and in this short story, Crane is no exception. It did not come from Crane's imagination. Rather, it stemmed from his personal experience. As a young war reporter, Crane was on his way from Florida to Cuba when his vessel, the *Commodore*, encountered a violent **tempest**. Within hours, the ship had sunk, leaving a few lucky survivors on a tiny lifeboat to be subjected to the fury of nature. Throughout the story, Crane depicts scene after scene as if they were snapshots or a short film of what the men in the boat were up against. Through his prose, Crane is able to reveal the unadulterated, brutal realism manifest in nature itself.

13 According to paragraph 2, *The Open Boat* is important as a naturalist work because

- Ⓐ it is a true account taken from Crane's own personal experience
- Ⓑ the story is completely fabricated from Crane's imagination
- Ⓒ it is based on a series of events in a shipwreck that Crane heard of
- Ⓓ it does not attempt to glorify Crane's heroism against nature

📖 Glossary
tempest: a violent rain and wind storm; a hurricane

³ ⇒ As Crane continues with the theme of man versus nature in *The Open Boat*, the element of pessimism, crucial to any naturalistic work, becomes quite apparent. The men are at the mercy of the storms and the seas and cannot do much to save themselves. In this sense, Crane reveals the indifference of nature and the universe in relation to the life or plight of human beings in general. It is obvious to him that angels will not swoop down and save the unfortunate men. The situation of the shipwreck is ideal because ordinary everyday people must face an extreme situation from which it is more than likely that they will perish. Crane continually creates a mood of impending doom and the punishing nature of the universe throughout the story. Along the way, he provides little commentary on the situation, forcing readers to place themselves immediately on the boat with the men while enforcing the dark tone of the story. But even to Crane and most naturalist writers, all is not lost.

14 The author discusses "nature" in paragraph 3 in order to

- Ⓐ show how Crane believes divine powers will save humanity
- Ⓑ note that nature itself is stronger than all of humankind
- Ⓒ indicate that nature does not care for strife among people
- Ⓓ reveal how it is pessimistic toward life on the Earth

15 According to paragraph 3, another element of Crane's style in *The Open Boat* is

- Ⓐ to put the reader in the midst of the plight of the characters
- Ⓑ to provide the reader with characters who have different opinions
- Ⓒ to keep the reader far removed from the actual plot of the story
- Ⓓ to confuse the reader by rendering complex metaphors

Though the outcome is bleak, Crane does add a glimmer of hope to the story. While in general, the individuals may seem insignificant in the grand scheme of the universe or to nature itself, Crane instills the importance of camaraderie in the story. In order to survive, the individuals in the boat must cooperate and help one another against the forces of nature. Together, they have some dominion of control over their fate, but less so individually. Though they are isolated out among the waves in sight of shore, they remain unified in their struggle for survival, which undermines the predominant pessimistic outlook of the story as a whole.

16. The word "they" in the passage refers to
    Ⓐ the individuals
    Ⓑ the individuals in the boat
    Ⓒ the forces of nature
    Ⓓ the waves

5 → While Crane's work *The Open Boat* is a dark account of a chance situation that turns fatal for many, but not all, of the crew of the *Commodore*, it also sets forth the main elements of a naturalistic literary work at the turn of the twentieth century. Despite the fact that nature can be unrelenting and compassionless toward humans at any given moment, Crane ultimately shows how individuals still always have the capacity to strive together to overcome hardships and disaster. Furthermore, the accuracy and detail by Crane shun any possibility of a sugarcoated reality and reveal the true ferocity of nature as it is.

17 The word "shun" in the passage is closest in meaning to
- Ⓐ reduce
- Ⓑ ignore
- Ⓒ avoid
- Ⓓ admit

18 According to paragraph 5, the men in the boat are significant because
- Ⓐ they show that by banding together, human beings can persevere
- Ⓑ they represent the ultimate downfall of life according to Crane
- Ⓒ they allow fate to run its course and to decide their own futures
- Ⓓ they discount nature and do not take it seriously until the end

Though the outcome is bleak, Crane does add a glimmer of hope to the story. While in general, the individuals may seem insignificant in the grand scheme of the universe or to nature itself, Crane instills the importance of camaraderie in the story. ■ In order to survive, the individuals in the boat must cooperate and help one another against the forces of nature. ■ Together, they have some dominion of control over their fate, but less so individually. ■ Though they are isolated out among the waves in sight of shore, they remain unified in their struggle for survival, which undermines the predominant pessimistic outlook of the story as a whole. ■

19 Look at the four squares [■] that indicate where the following sentence could be added to the passage.

For instance, all the sailors cast their ranks aside and help each other swim to shore for safety.

Where would the sentence best fit?

Click on a square [■] to add the sentence to the passage.

20 Directions: An introductory sentence for a brief summary of the passage is provided below. Complete the summary by selecting the THREE answer choices that express the most important ideas of the passage. Some sentences do not belong because they express ideas that are not presented in the passage or are minor ideas in the passage. **This question is worth 2 points.**

Drag your answer choices to the spaces where they belong.
To remove an answer choice, click on it. To review the passage, click on **View Text**.

Stephen Crane's work *The Open Boat* is an important naturalist work that shows the ruthlessness of nature.

-
-
-

Answer Choices

1. In the story, Crane attempts to interject his own religious beliefs at times.

2. Crane's specific choice of subject matter supports it as a naturalistic work.

3. Hope has no role in Crane's short story *The Open Boat*.

4. In Crane's view, nature is insensitive to the struggle of human beings.

5. Crane warns that the isolation of an individual is a dangerous tactic.

6. As a young reporter, Crane began a journey to the island of Cuba.

How to Master Skills for the TOEFL® iBT

Actual Test
READING 2

09

TOEFL READING

Reading Section Directions

This section measures your ability to understand academic passages in English. You will have **35 minutes** to read and answer questions about **2 passages**. A clock at the top of the screen will show you how much time is remaining.

Most questions are worth 1 point but the last question for each passage is worth more than 1 point. The directions for the last question indicate how many points you may receive.

Some passages include a word or phrase that is **underlined** in blue. Click on the word or phrase to see a definition or an explanation.

When you want to move to the next question, click on **Next**. You may skip questions and go back to them later. If you want to return to previous questions, click on **Back**. You can click on **Review** at any time, and the review screen will show you which questions you have answered and which you have not answered. From this review screen, you may go directly to any question you have already seen in the Reading section.

Click on **Continue** to go on.

Early Navigation

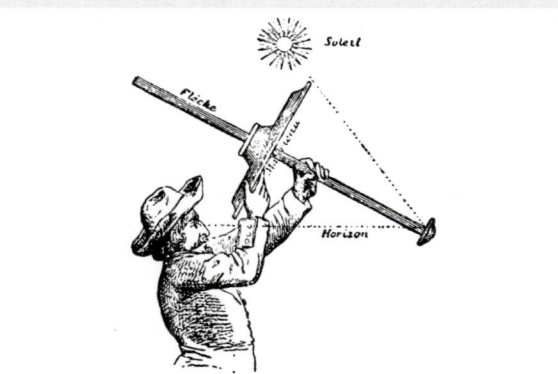

A navigator using a back-staff

    For early mariners, losing sight of land was usually an unnerving event; therefore, numerous forms of navigational techniques were invented and implemented by sailors. While the compass was probably the most common instrument used by the first sailors to traverse the oceans, it was by no means the only helpful one. Another rudimentary, though effective, instrument relied upon was called the cross-staff. It was used to measure angles between the horizon and the sun or other stars to calculate the latitudinal position of the ship. Additionally, because the compass gave a general or estimated position in relation to the magnetic north pole, which was always shifting, the implementation of the cross-staff in combination with the compass often helped refine a ship's position. For many years, it was an invaluable tool on risky ocean voyages, which lacked the luxury of landmarks or maps.

    The construction and design of the cross-staff was a simplistic one. It consisted of two wooden staffs, one longer and the other a shorter crosspiece, which slid up and down the main piece. The larger staff also had a numeric scale etched or inscribed into it for important calculating purposes. Sailors would incorporate the cross-staff with their vision and the direction of the sun at given times of the day. Typically, it was used during sunrise, at noon, and at sunset, which denote east, south, and west, respectively. Thus, sailors were able to calculate the elevation of the sun in its various stages and to estimate their latitude, which is the angular distance of any given point north or south of the equator.

    The ease of use of the cross-staff helped navigators plot the latitudinal location of their ships in degrees. First, one end of the cross-staff was held up to the eye of the sailor as the crosspiece was slid and adjusted up and down the cross-staff at right angles until the upper edge of the crosspiece lined up with the sun or a star and the horizon. That is, it occupied the space between the two distinct points. At this stage, the point on the shaft's scale was recorded and converted into degrees for their general position at that moment. In addition, different sizes of crosspieces were incorporated depending on the ship's distance from the equator. For example, if the ship was in close proximity to the equator, a shorter piece was used because the North Star appeared closer to the horizon. As the ship moved to the north, the gap between the North Star and the horizon widened and therefore required an adjustment in the size of the crosspiece.

Despite its simplicity and effectiveness, the cross-staff still had its share of drawbacks. The primary one was the sun itself. Early navigators had to look directly at the sun in order to produce an accurate measurement; this often permanently damaged their vision. In order to compensate for or to alleviate this issue, an improved version of the cross-staff, appropriately named the back-staff, was created. Essentially, the back-staff worked by the same principles as the cross-staff, yet its design was altered to make it more user friendly. The back-staff employed an arched sliding piece that allowed the navigator to stand with his back to the sun while the sun cast a shadow via the arch onto the main staff. The spot where the shadow fell was noted, recorded, and later calculated into a degrees latitude position. The navigator did not have to look directly into the sun's scorching rays but could still make an accurate reading.

Some of the earliest navigational aids, such as the cross-staff and the back-staff, helped ship officers establish the general latitudinal position of their ships. They were easy to use and fairly efficient, yet they were by no means exact. Captains and navigators still had to factor in a number of other variables, such as wind speed, currents, and tides, to determine their positions more precisely. Nevertheless, as a basic instrument for getting from point A to point B in the least amount of danger, the cross-staff proved to be an invaluable tool for navigation when ships first began to venture away from the safety of the shores.

Early Navigation

1 → For early mariners, losing sight of land was usually an unnerving event; therefore, numerous forms of navigational techniques were invented and implemented by sailors. While the compass was probably the most common instrument used by the first sailors to traverse the oceans, it was by no means the only helpful one. Another rudimentary, though effective, instrument relied upon was called the cross-staff. It was used to measure angles between the horizon and the sun or other stars to calculate the latitudinal position of the ship. Additionally, because the compass gave a general or estimated position in relation to the magnetic north pole, which was always shifting, the implementation of the cross-staff in combination with the compass often helped refine a ship's position. For many years, it was an invaluable tool on risky ocean voyages, which lacked the luxury of landmarks or maps.

1. The word "traverse" in the passage is closest in meaning to
   - A) challenge
   - B) discover
   - C) understand
   - D) cross

2. The author discusses the "compass" in paragraph 1 in order to
   - A) show how no other early navigational instrument rivaled it
   - B) indicate how its accuracy improved when used with the cross-staff
   - C) contrast it with the way in which the cross-staff was used with the sun
   - D) suggest that while popular, numerous other aids were more effective

The construction and design of the cross-staff was a simplistic one. It consisted of two wooden staffs, one longer and the other a shorter crosspiece, which slid up and down the main piece. The larger staff also had a numeric scale etched or inscribed into it for important calculating purposes. Sailors would incorporate the cross-staff with their vision and the direction of the sun at given times of the day. Typically, it was used during sunrise, at noon, and at sunset, which denote east, south, and west, respectively. Thus, sailors were able to calculate the elevation of the sun in its various stages and to estimate their latitude, which is the angular distance of any given point north or south of the equator.

3. The word "it" in the passage refers to
   - (A) the cross-staff
   - (B) a shorter crosspiece
   - (C) the larger staff
   - (D) a numeric scale

4. Which of the sentences below best expresses the essential information in the highlighted sentence in the passage? *Incorrect* answer choices change the meaning in important ways or leave out essential information.
   - (A) Sailors could figure out how high the sun was and then guess their latitude, which showed where they were in relation to the equator.
   - (B) By measuring their angular distance from the equator, sailors were able to know where the sun was located in the sky.
   - (C) Sailors could guess how far away they were from the equator since the height of the sun told them their relative latitude.
   - (D) Sailors could judge their latitude in relation to the equator, which then enabled them to determine the elevation of the sun.

³ ➡ The ease of use of the cross-staff helped navigators plot the latitudinal location of their ships in degrees. First, one end of the cross-staff was held up to the eye of the sailor as the crosspiece was slid and adjusted up and down the cross-staff at right angles until the upper edge of the crosspiece lined up with the sun or a star and the horizon. That is, it occupied the space between the two distinct points. At this stage, the point on the shaft's scale was recorded and converted into degrees for their general position at that moment. In addition, different sizes of crosspieces were incorporated depending on the ship's distance from the equator. For example, if the ship was in close proximity to the equator, a shorter piece was used because the North Star appeared closer to the horizon. As the ship moved to the north, the gap between the North Star and the horizon widened and therefore required an adjustment in the size of the crosspiece.

5. According to paragraph 3, which of the following is true of the cross-staff?

   Ⓐ It consisted of two staffs of equal length that were placed to the sailor's eye.
   Ⓑ It had a scale that listed various degrees on the main part of the apparatus.
   Ⓒ It could not be used effectively if the North Star was too close to the horizon.
   Ⓓ Its crosspiece was crucial for measuring the distance between the sun and the horizon.

6. According to paragraph 3, a smaller crosspiece was used because

   Ⓐ the ship was nearer the equator and the North Star was further away
   Ⓑ as the ship sailed north, the gap between the North Star and horizon opened
   Ⓒ the North Star was closer to the horizon when the ship approached the equator
   Ⓓ the space between the horizon and North Star could be measured with it at any time

4 → Despite its simplicity and effectiveness, the cross-staff still had its share of drawbacks. The primary one was the sun itself. Early navigators had to look directly at the sun in order to produce an accurate measurement; this often permanently damaged their vision. In order to compensate for or to alleviate this issue, an improved version of the cross-staff, appropriately named the back-staff, was created. Essentially, the back-staff worked by the same principles as the cross-staff, yet its design was altered to make it more user friendly. The back-staff employed an arched sliding piece that allowed the navigator to stand with his back to the sun while the sun cast a shadow via the arch onto the main staff. The spot where the shadow fell was noted, recorded, and later calculated into a degrees latitude position. The navigator did not have to look directly into the sun's scorching rays but could still make an accurate reading.

Some of the earliest navigational aids, such as the cross-staff and the back-staff, helped ship officers establish the general latitudinal position of their ships. They were easy to use and fairly efficient, yet they were by no means exact. Captains and navigators still had to factor in a number of other variables, such as wind speed, currents, and tides, to determine their positions more precisely. Nevertheless, as a basic instrument for getting from point A to point B in the least amount of danger, the cross-staff proved to be an invaluable tool for navigation when ships first began to venture away from the safety of the shores.

7. According to paragraph 4, why was the back-staff developed?
   - Ⓐ To implement a better scaling system into the original design of the staff
   - Ⓑ To help sailors avoid direct contact with the sun for better positioning
   - Ⓒ To use shadows instead of a crosspiece for more efficient measurement
   - Ⓓ To allow navigators to look at the staff for a longer period of time

8. The word "precisely" in the passage is closest in meaning to
   - Ⓐ reasonably
   - Ⓑ accurately
   - Ⓒ carefully
   - Ⓓ vaguely

Despite its simplicity and effectiveness, the cross-staff still had its share of drawbacks. The primary one was the sun itself. Early navigators had to look directly at the sun in order to produce an accurate measurement; this often permanently damaged their vision. In order to compensate for or to alleviate this issue, an improved version of the cross-staff, appropriately named the back-staff, was created. Essentially, the back-staff worked by the same principles as the cross-staff, yet its design was altered to make it more user friendly. ■ The back-staff employed an arched sliding piece that allowed the navigator to stand with his back to the sun while the sun cast a shadow via the arch onto the main staff. ■ The spot where the shadow fell was noted, recorded, and later calculated into a degrees latitude position. ■ The navigator did not have to look directly into the sun's scorching rays but could still make an accurate reading. ■

10 Directions: An introductory sentence for a brief summary of the passage is provided below. Complete the summary by selecting the THREE answer choices that express the most important ideas of the passage. Some sentences do not belong because they express ideas that are not presented in the passage or are minor ideas in the passage. **This question is worth 2 points.**

Drag your answer choices to the spaces where they belong.
To remove an answer choice, click on it. To review the passage, click on **View Text**.

Because of early navigational aids such as the cross-staff, mariners could judge their latitudinal position more accurately.

-
-
-

Answer Choices

1. The back-staff protected sailors' eyes from the sun's harmful rays.

2. Without instruments such as the cross-staff, sailors could have become lost.

3. The compass was actually not as common as the cross-staff or the back-staff.

4. The angle of the sun in relation to the horizon established a ship's latitude.

5. The cross-staff used three crosspieces of different sizes for measurements.

6. The cross-staff made sailors less reliant upon the North Star for navigation.

Stem Cell Sources

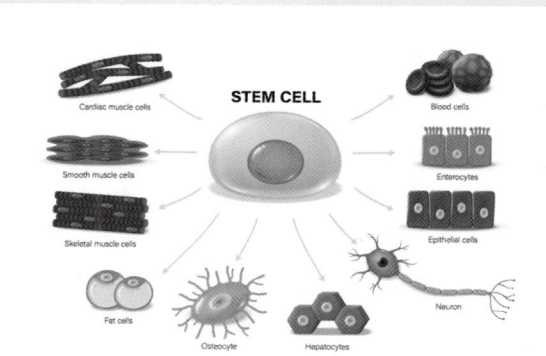

Stem cell differentiation into various cell types

    The new miracle of the medical world is the stem cell, a marvel of human nature in that it can become any of nearly 220 cell types that constitute the human body. It is often called a blank cell that can be programmed to become other cells. Researchers predict that by using stem cells, they can create organs that can be transplanted into people who desperately need them to save their lives. The most common source of stem cells is the human embryo, the initial stage of human life after a female egg is impregnated by a male sperm. In this very fact lies an ethical **conundrum** that has rocked both the medical and political landscape of the United States and other countries. Coupled with this is new research in cloning, which has seen some success in developing animal species without the use of normal birthing procedures. These areas of research are making quite a few people nervous about both the sources of stem cells and where the research is taking mankind.

    Most stem cell-containing embryos come from four different sources: fertility clinics, which often store more human embryos than are needed; fetuses from unwanted pregnancies that are aborted; therapeutic cloning, which is when a human egg is stimulated into an embryo-like state; and custom-fertilization, in which a human egg is deliberately fertilized with sperm to create an embryo in order to harvest its stem cells. Morally, many people are outraged by these sources, claiming that human life is not something that should be tampered with and created just for scientific and medical purposes. At the core of this debate is the issue of what really constitutes a human being with one side claiming a human does not exist until born from its mother while the other side declares that once egg and sperm meet, life has begun.

    The United States government has taken an active role in the debate and is consciously looking at the voting booth while making decisions regarding stem cell research. The government gave the go-ahead for federal spending on stem cell research but limited activity to specimens that already existed, which means that no new embryos could be created solely for stem cell research. Similar laws regarding cloning research, including therapeutic cloning, have been proposed. Many universities and research centers worry that these laws may cause their best and brightest scientists to seek appointments overseas, where stem cell research is not so controversial.

Scientists now seek non-embryonic sources of stem cells to avoid the controversy in the future and to allow them to carry out their work without interference. Unfortunately, so far, the search has not unearthed any sources as perfect as human embryo stem cells. Research suggests that inside each person there is a limited supply of stem cells in the blood that are used to repair red blood cells when they are damaged. Some scientists believe they might be able to harvest these cells, but results so far have had limited success in extracting and using them to produce other cells. Even the limited successes they have had are being questioned by other experts as unproven. Two other sources, baby teeth and adult bone marrow, show some possibilities, but again the research is being questioned, and as of yet, no positive new source of stem cells has been found to replace human embryos.

In view of the ethical debate that surrounds stem cell research, especially its sources of stem cells, it will likely be some time before the entire issue is laid to rest. Meanwhile, countless people suffer from illnesses that could be cured or their pain alleviated by the work that comes from stem cell research. Some people believe the debate about when human life actually begins needs to take a backseat to the issue of when human life will end, especially when it is possible to save someone from an early death. In the end, the research will likely get done in a place that puts existing human life above that in the embryonic state. It is also highly unlikely that that place will be the United States.

Glossary

conundrum: something which is puzzling to solve

Stem Cell Sources

1 → The new miracle of the medical world is the stem cell, a marvel of human nature in that it can become any of nearly 220 cell types that constitute the human body. It is often called a blank cell that can be programmed to become other cells. Researchers predict that by using stem cells, they can create organs that can be transplanted into people who desperately need them to save their lives. The most common source of stem cells is the human embryo, the initial stage of human life after a female egg is impregnated by a male sperm. In this very fact lies an ethical **conundrum** that has rocked both the medical and political landscape of the United States and other countries. Coupled with this is new research in cloning, which has seen some success in developing animal species without the use of normal birthing procedures. These areas of research are making quite a few people nervous about both the sources of stem cells and where the research is taking mankind.

11 The word "constitute" in the passage is closest in meaning to
  Ⓐ form
  Ⓑ cure
  Ⓒ contain
  Ⓓ sustain

12 According to paragraph 1, a stem cell is unlike other cells because
  Ⓐ it has at least 220 different parts
  Ⓑ it can develop into any other cell
  Ⓒ it has been used to cure illnesses
  Ⓓ it is at the center of a controversy

📖 Glossary
conundrum: something which is puzzling to solve

2 → Most stem cell-containing embryos come from four different sources: fertility clinics, which often store more human embryos than are needed; fetuses from unwanted pregnancies that are aborted; therapeutic cloning, which is when a human egg is stimulated into an embryo-like state; and custom-fertilization, in which a human egg is deliberately fertilized with sperm to create an embryo in order to harvest its stem cells. Morally, many people are outraged by these sources, claiming that human life is not something that should be tampered with and created just for scientific and medical purposes. At the core of this debate is the issue of what really constitutes a human being with one side claiming a human does not exist until born from its mother while the other side declares that once egg and sperm meet, life has begun.

13 In paragraph 2, the author mentions all of the following as sources of stem cells EXCEPT:

(A) Embryos made for people who cannot conceive
(B) Human eggs that act like they are fertilized
(C) Artificially impregnated women
(D) The remains of unwanted babies

14 According to paragraph 2, the main debate concerning stem cell sources revolves around

(A) how they are extracted from the source
(B) what the stem cells are used for
(C) the methods used to produce them
(D) when someone believes life begins

³ ➡ The United States government has taken an active role in the debate and is consciously looking at the voting booth while making decisions regarding stem cell research. The government gave the go-ahead for federal spending on stem cell research but limited activity to specimens that already existed, which means that no new embryos could be created solely for stem cell research. Similar laws regarding cloning research, including therapeutic cloning, have been proposed. Many universities and research centers worry that these laws may cause their best and brightest scientists to seek appointments overseas, where stem cell research is not so controversial.

15 Which of the sentences below best expresses the essential information in the highlighted sentence in the passage? *Incorrect* answer choices change the meaning in important ways or leave out essential information.

Ⓐ The United States government is involved in the debate on stem cells only because it is worried about the voters.

Ⓑ The voters are making the United States government worried about its position on stem cell research.

Ⓒ The issue of stem cell research is one that most United States voters are concerned about.

Ⓓ The United States government's decisions on stem cell research reflect what its voting public wants.

16 According to paragraph 3, American universities and research institutes are worried about

Ⓐ not getting enough funds for stem cell research

Ⓑ losing people to better opportunities elsewhere

Ⓒ having the government shut down their operations

Ⓓ having to obtain new sources of stem cells

5 → In view of the ethical debate that surrounds stem cell research, especially its sources of stem cells, it will likely be some time before the entire issue is laid to rest. Meanwhile, countless people suffer from illnesses that could be cured or their pain alleviated by the work that comes from stem cell research. Some people believe the debate about when human life actually begins needs to take a backseat to the issue of when human life will end, especially when it is possible to save someone from an early death. In the end, the research will likely get done in a place that puts existing human life above that in the embryonic state. It is also highly unlikely that that place will be the United States.

17 The word "alleviated" in the passage is closest in meaning to
- Ⓐ lessened
- Ⓑ stopped
- Ⓒ released
- Ⓓ repaired

18 It can be inferred from paragraph 5 that stem cell research in some countries
- Ⓐ has as many difficulties as in the United States
- Ⓑ is seen primarily from a scientific, not moral, viewpoint
- Ⓒ has not made as much progress as in the United States
- Ⓓ is currently being used in the treatment of ill people

■ Scientists now seek non-embryonic sources of stem cells to avoid the controversy in the future and to allow them to carry out their work without interference. ■ Unfortunately, so far, the search has not unearthed any sources as perfect as human embryo stem cells. ■ Research suggests that inside each person there is a limited supply of stem cells in the blood that are used to repair red blood cells when they are damaged. ■ Some scientists believe they might be able to harvest these cells, but results so far have had limited success in extracting and using them to produce other cells. Even the limited successes they have had are being questioned by other experts as unproven. Two other sources, baby teeth and adult bone marrow, show some possibilities, but again the research is being questioned, and as of yet, no positive new source of stem cells has been found to replace human embryos.

19 Look at the four squares [■] that indicate where the following sentence could be added to the passage.

The main reason they are not perfect is that while embryo stem cells can become any other cell, other stem cells from different sources can only become limited types of cells.

Where would the sentence best fit?

Click on a square [■] to add the sentence to the passage.

20 Directions: An introductory sentence for a brief summary of the passage is provided below. Complete the summary by selecting the THREE answer choices that express the most important ideas of the passage. Some sentences do not belong because they express ideas that are not presented in the passage or are minor ideas in the passage. **This question is worth 2 points.**

Drag your answer choices to the spaces where they belong.
To remove an answer choice, click on it. To review the passage, click on **View Text**.

Stem cell research shows promise, but it has been hindered by the government in the United States.

-
-
-

Answer Choices

1. The necessity of finding new stem cell sources has slowed the progress of the stem cell research currently being conducted.

2. The United States government has passed laws that regulate stem cell research by limiting it to existing embryonic sources.

3. In many countries, stem cell research is advancing faster than the research being conducted in the United States.

4. Many people are upset that stem cells are taken from aborted fetuses and that human embryos are created simply to extract stem cells.

5. There is concern that the cloning of humans may be a final result of stem cell research since one method of stem cell creation involves cloning.

6. The slow progress of American stem cell research can lead some experts to seek postings in other countries to conduct research in better circumstances.

How to Master Skills for the TOEFL® iBT

Actual Test
READING 2

10

TOEFL READING

Reading Section Directions

This section measures your ability to understand academic passages in English. You will have **35 minutes** to read and answer questions about **2 passages**. A clock at the top of the screen will show you how much time is remaining.

Most questions are worth 1 point but the last question for each passage is worth more than 1 point. The directions for the last question indicate how many points you may receive.

Some passages include a word or phrase that is **underlined** in blue. Click on the word or phrase to see a definition or an explanation.

When you want to move to the next question, click on **Next**. You may skip questions and go back to them later. If you want to return to previous questions, click on **Back**. You can click on **Review** at any time, and the review screen will show you which questions you have answered and which you have not answered. From this review screen, you may go directly to any question you have already seen in the Reading section.

Click on **Continue** to go on.

The War of 1812

The *USS Constitution*, a key warship in the War of 1812

    The War of 1812, which lasted around three years, is more of an afterthought in most histories of the United States and England. England dominated the naval battles on the seas and was even able to take the capital of the United States, Washington, D.C., and burn the White House. For the United States, it had a few major victories during the course of the war, including doing well to disrupt British influence in the Caribbean. Overall, however, neither country ever really gained anything substantial. It was mostly a war fought on account of principles the U.S. believed England had violated too many times. There were a few major causes of the War of 1812, but mostly, it was a result of maritime actions by England against American ships. The United States' invasion of British-controlled Canada at the start of the war was a bold yet **crass** move. At the time, the English navy and infantry easily outnumbered the fragmented, tiny American side.

    The first main cause of the war between the U.S. and England was a political one. The leaders of the U.S. realized they could not defeat the huge English military, but England was already busy fighting a war against the French in Europe. England continued to meddle in American commerce and treat the country much like a colony; therefore, the Americans believed the time was ripe to make a statement despite not actually expecting to defeat the entire British Empire. Tensions between the two countries were increasing for years leading up to the war; however, many see the American move to war as poorly calculated for two reasons. First, the American military was small and untested, and second, the British military was the complete opposite—massive and proven. Still, due to provoking maritime acts by England, the Americans felt they had no choice but to wage war.

    The British had several reasons for their actions on the seas with a major one being that they felt threatened by American shipping and commerce. While war continued between England and France, American ships benefited by supplying the French with greatly needed supplies, which angered the British. The Americans were therefore aiding the enemy in the eyes of the British. Simultaneously, the United States was also prospering economically from it. Because England considered itself the ruler of the seas, it felt threatened by the Americans. Further blockades by the British allowed them to gain greater control of the oceans. The Americans regarded the intervention of British naval forces as a violation of international maritime law, yet the British continued their tactics to weaken France and to bolster their sea trade dominance and even took steps that harmed American shipping.

Another crucial reason for the War of 1812 was the issue of impressment, the forcing of individuals against their free will into public service like military service. It also involves the seizing of property. England exercised impressment on sailors on American ships, which created outrage in the American public. In many instances, British ships stopped and boarded American merchant ships, ostensibly looking for deserters from the British military. At their own discretion, British captains frequently seized naturalized Americans as well as citizens born in the United States and then forced them to fight in the war in Europe. To the government as well as the American public, these actions were unacceptable, so there was outrage in the United States. First, it was unlawful, and second, England was again treating the United States like a servant of the crown. The issue of impressment was probably the most heated subject of any other concerning the War of 1812.

There are numerous other causes of the War of 1812. The British mistreated neutral American ships and men. They also ignored the sovereignty of the United States and many of its citizens. Though outmanned, the Americans sent a strong message to England by challenging its military. Ultimately, each country signed terms of peace to end the war in 1815. The Americans also proved that they would not back down from any threats to their freedom and showed how they would not allow any country to create its own rules or to ignore established international treaties.

Glossary
crass: stupid or foolish

The War of 1812

1 → The War of 1812, which lasted around three years, is more of an afterthought in most histories of the United States and England. England dominated the naval battles on the seas and was even able to take the capital of the United States, Washington, D.C., and burn the White House. For the United States, it had a few major victories during the course of the war, including doing well to disrupt British influence in the Caribbean. Overall, however, neither country ever really gained anything substantial. It was mostly a war fought on account of principles the U.S. believed England had violated too many times. There were a few major causes of the War of 1812, but mostly, it was a result of maritime actions by England against American ships. The United States' invasion of British-controlled Canada at the start of the war was a bold yet **crass** move. At the time, the English navy and infantry easily outnumbered the fragmented, tiny American side.

1. The word "disrupt" in the passage is closest in meaning to
   - Ⓐ dismiss
   - Ⓑ disturb
   - Ⓒ distinguish
   - Ⓓ distort

2. According to paragraph 1, which of the following is true of the War of 1812?
   - Ⓐ The British won every naval encounter with the Americans.
   - Ⓑ The war began because the United States invaded Canada.
   - Ⓒ The two countries' militaries were fairly evenly matched.
   - Ⓓ The war ended without Britain or the United States gaining much.

Glossary
crass: stupid or foolish

2 → The first main cause of the war between the U.S. and England was a political one. The leaders of the U.S. realized they could not defeat the huge English military, but England was already busy fighting a war against the French in Europe. England continued to meddle in American commerce and treat the country much like a colony; therefore, the Americans believed the time was ripe to make a statement despite not actually expecting to defeat the entire British Empire. Tensions between the two countries were increasing for years leading up to the war; however, many see the American move to war as poorly calculated for two reasons. First, the American military was small and untested, and second, the British military was the complete opposite—massive and proven. Still, due to provoking maritime acts by England, the Americans felt they had no choice but to wage war.

3. Which of the sentences below best expresses the essential information in the highlighted sentence in the passage? *Incorrect* answer choices change the meaning in important ways or leave out essential information.
   - Ⓐ The U.S. believed England was breaking maritime law during the war.
   - Ⓑ The British did not want to fight the U.S. in any naval battles.
   - Ⓒ The U.S. avoided a war against England for as long as it could.
   - Ⓓ British transgressions ultimately forced the U.S. to go to war.

4. According to paragraph 2, why did the Americans go to war with England?
   - Ⓐ They believed their military was stronger than that of England.
   - Ⓑ They wanted to make a strong statement to England.
   - Ⓒ They thought England was too busy fighting against France.
   - Ⓓ They felt the British Empire was too large to attack them back quickly.

³ ⇒ The British had several reasons for their actions on the seas with a major one being that they felt threatened by American shipping and commerce. While war continued between England and France, American ships benefited by supplying the French with greatly needed supplies, which angered the British. The Americans were therefore aiding the enemy in the eyes of the British. Simultaneously, the United States was also prospering economically from it. Because England considered itself the ruler of the seas, it felt threatened by the Americans. Further blockades by the British allowed them to gain greater control of the oceans. The Americans regarded the intervention of British naval forces as a violation of international maritime law, yet the British continued their tactics to weaken France and to bolster their sea trade dominance and even took steps that harmed American shipping.

5. The author discusses "further blockades" in paragraph 3 in order to
    A) show how England was able to counteract U.S. policy
    B) contrast British and American naval tactics during the war
    C) note how the British abided by international laws at all times
    D) indicate the main method Britain used to defend against France

6. Which of the following can be inferred from paragraph 3 about France?
    A) It had a stronger infantry than the British.
    B) It was not concerned with territory in the U.S.
    C) It was on better terms with the U.S. than England.
    D) It used the Americans to invade the British Isles.

4 → Another crucial reason for the War of 1812 was the issue of impressment, the forcing of individuals against their free will into public service like military service. It also involves the seizing of property. England exercised impressment on sailors on American ships, which created outrage in the American public. In many instances, British ships stopped and boarded American merchant ships, ostensibly looking for deserters from the British military. At their own discretion, British captains frequently seized naturalized Americans as well as citizens born in the United States and then forced them to fight in the war in Europe. To the government as well as the American public, these actions were unacceptable, so there was outrage in the United States. First, it was unlawful, and second, England was again treating the United States like a servant of the crown. The issue of impressment was probably the most heated subject of any other concerning the War of 1812.

7. According to paragraph 4, which of the following is NOT true of impressment?

   Ⓐ England used it to increase its military.
   Ⓑ The Americans also used it against the British.
   Ⓒ The Americans disagreed with the practice.
   Ⓓ It affected sailors other than just deserters.

5 → There are numerous other causes of the War of 1812. ■ The British mistreated neutral American ships and men. ■ They also ignored the sovereignty of the United States and many of its citizens. ■ Though outmanned, the Americans sent a strong message to England by challenging its military. ■ Ultimately, each country signed terms of peace to end the war in 1815. The Americans also proved that they would not back down from any threats to their freedom and showed how they would not allow any country to create its own rules or to ignore established international treaties.

8. According to paragraph 5, which of the following is true of the War of 1812?
   Ⓐ The United States ultimately lost the war.
   Ⓑ The British were the biggest losers of the war.
   Ⓒ The U.S. established what it set out to do.
   Ⓓ The Americans were more at fault for the war.

9. Look at the four squares [■] that indicate where the following sentence could be added to the passage.

   But most of the blame can be laid on England.

   Where would the sentence best fit?

   Click on a square [■] to add the sentence to the passage.

10 Directions: An introductory sentence for a brief summary of the passage is provided below. Complete the summary by selecting the THREE answer choices that express the most important ideas of the passage. Some sentences do not belong because they express ideas that are not presented in the passage or are minor ideas in the passage. **This question is worth 2 points.**

Drag your answer choices to the spaces where they belong.
To remove an answer choice, click on it. To review the passage, click on **View Text**.

Because of England's naval transgressions, the United States had no choice but to declare war in 1812.

-
-
-

Answer Choices

1. England disregarded the right of freedom of many U.S. sailors.
2. The United States' military was much smaller than England's.
3. Relations between England and the U.S. were good until the war.
4. England used impressment to force U.S. citizens to fight its war.
5. England was able to capture Washington and burned the White House.
6. American ships aided France with valuable supplies and benefited from doing that.

The Evolution of Stars

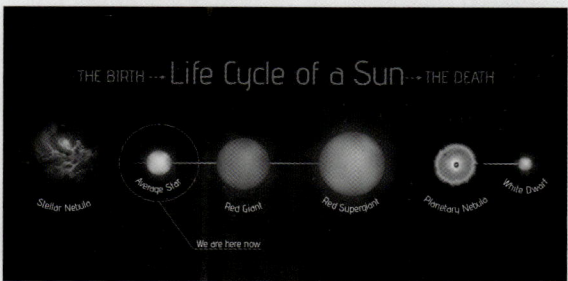

The life cycle of a star

   Much like living organisms on the Earth, stars also experience evolution over time. In essence, they exhibit certain qualities when they are young as well as when they are much older. They continuously evolve and are born out of a nebula, a large mass of clouds in a galaxy. From time to time, these cloud masses begin to collapse, and their internal density starts to increase, possibly due to the presence of a neighboring supernova, a rare astronomical phenomenon that occurs when a star explodes or a future star's galaxy spins. As gas and dust particles continue to collide and accelerate, heat increases, and a core starts forming. A star in an early stage of evolution is called a main sequence star. Millions or billions of years later, it can become a giant or a supergiant.

   Main sequence stars are relatively young and small. The majority of known stars are main sequence stars as they account for about 85% of all stars. Additionally, their brightness, or illumination, compared to late-stage stars is not as great or intense. They rely on nuclear fission for energy by converting hydrogen, their main source of fuel, into helium. Earth's own sun is a prime example of a main sequence star, which can be classified further depending on the star's special characteristics. The sun is considered a yellow dwarf star due to its age, size, and, of course, color. According to scientists, the sun is about 4.5 billion years old and has so far utilized half of the hydrogen fuel at its core.

   In the core of a yellow star such as the sun, protons fuse together due to extreme levels of heat to create helium nuclei. During the process, some energy is released. As the fusion of hydrogen continues, outward radiation relieves the internal pressure within the star, making it somewhat more stable as any further collapse of the star ceases. Eventually, yellow stars will sap their source of energy and enter their next major stage of evolution as giant or supergiant stars. These stars have entered the golden years of their existence—the more mature years of their lives—which does not necessarily mean they are becoming sedentary.

Giant and supergiant stars are examples of some of the oldest and largest stars discovered. Most continue to expand and are between ten to one hundred times larger than the diameter of the sun. Furthermore, their heat is more intense than the younger yellow dwarfs as it typically reaches between 2,500 to 3,500 degrees Celsius. There are three general subcategories of giant stars: blue giants, red giants, and supergiants. Blue giants are the most extreme on the heat scale of any star, and supergiants, while quite rare, are the largest known stars with some being as enormous as an entire solar system. Ultimately, most common stars pass through the red giant stage in their evolution as their hydrogen fuel source becomes depleted in their helium core's outer shell. In turn, the core begins to heat up rapidly, causing the outer layers of the shell's gases to expand outwardly and to cool to some degree. Internally, the pressure becomes relieved, and the drop in temperature gives the star its characteristic red hue.

Not all stars pass through identical stages as the others. The evolution of each star is dependent on numerous factors, including its specific gaseous makeup and the gravitational forces affecting it. The birth-mass of the star is another crucial factor in a star's development. The greater a star's mass, the more quickly it is able to fuse hydrogen into helium. Moreover, increased helium production can cause the core of the star to contract further as it, in essence, feeds more and more on hydrogen. Once completely depleted of hydrogen, a red giant's core of helium begins to combust, or burn, causing major instability with the inner core and the outer portions of the star and releasing most of its shells of gaseous energy into the surrounding region again as a nebula. Still, at its center are the remnants of the star, essentially the core itself, called a white dwarf, which is one of the final stages of a main sequence star's evolution.

The Evolution of Stars

1 ➡ Much like living organisms on the Earth, stars also experience evolution over time. In essence, they exhibit certain qualities when they are young as well as when they are much older. They continuously evolve and are born out of a nebula, a large mass of clouds in a galaxy. From time to time, these cloud masses begin to collapse, and their internal density starts to increase, possibly due to the presence of a neighboring supernova, a rare astronomical phenomenon that occurs when a star explodes or a future star's galaxy spins. As gas and dust particles continue to collide and accelerate, heat increases, and a core starts forming. A star in an early stage of evolution is called a main sequence star. Millions or billions of years later, it can become a giant or a supergiant.

11 According to paragraph 1, which of the following is true of stars?
- Ⓐ They are created when a supernova contracts and explodes.
- Ⓑ Their characteristics change over the course of time.
- Ⓒ Gaseous nebulae are necessary for stars to form in galaxies.
- Ⓓ Stars have the same traits when they are young and old.

2 → Main sequence stars are relatively young and small. The majority of known stars are main sequence stars as they account for about 85% of all stars. Additionally, their brightness, or illumination, compared to late-stage stars is not as great or intense. They rely on nuclear fission for energy by converting hydrogen, their main source of fuel, into helium. Earth's own sun is a prime example of a main sequence star, which can be classified further depending on the star's special characteristics. The sun is considered a yellow dwarf star due to its age, size, and, of course, color. According to scientists, the sun is about 4.5 billion years old and has so far utilized half of the hydrogen fuel at its core.

12 The author discusses "hydrogen" in paragraph 2 in order to

- (A) contrast main sequence stars with smaller yellow dwarf stars
- (B) show how main sequence stars are able to create their energy
- (C) note that it is more crucial to nuclear fission than helium
- (D) indicate that eighty-five percent of a star's makeup is composed of hydrogen

3 → In the core of a yellow star such as the sun, protons fuse together due to extreme levels of heat to create helium nuclei. During the process, some energy is released. As the fusion of hydrogen continues, outward radiation relieves the internal pressure within the star, making it somewhat more stable as any further collapse of the star ceases. Eventually, yellow stars will sap their source of energy and enter their next major stage of evolution as giant or supergiant stars. These stars have entered the golden years of their existence—the more mature years of their lives—which does not necessarily mean they are becoming sedentary.

13. According to paragraphs 2 and 3, which of the following is NOT true of yellow stars?
   - Ⓐ They run out of energy after some time.
   - Ⓑ They may eventually become giant stars.
   - Ⓒ They can convert helium into hydrogen.
   - Ⓓ They can release a huge amount of energy.

14. The word "sedentary" in the passage is closest in meaning to
   - Ⓐ lifeless
   - Ⓑ inactive
   - Ⓒ functional
   - Ⓓ complex

Giant and supergiant stars are examples of some of the oldest and largest stars discovered. Most continue to expand and are between ten to one hundred times larger than the diameter of the sun. Furthermore, their heat is more intense than the younger yellow dwarfs as it typically reaches between 2,500 to 3,500 degrees Celsius. There are three general subcategories of giant stars: blue giants, red giants, and supergiants. Blue giants are the most extreme on the heat scale of any star, and supergiants, while quite rare, are the largest known stars with some being as enormous as an entire solar system. Ultimately, most common stars pass through the red giant stage in their evolution as their hydrogen fuel source becomes depleted in their helium core's outer shell. In turn, the core begins to heat up rapidly, causing the outer layers of the shell's gases to expand outwardly and to cool to some degree. Internally, the pressure becomes relieved, and the drop in temperature gives the star its characteristic red hue.

15 Which of the sentences below best expresses the essential information in the highlighted sentence in the passage? *Incorrect* answer choices change the meaning in important ways or leave out essential information.

- Ⓐ The shell's gases are pushed out by the cooling of the core.
- Ⓑ The core begins to expand and cool while losing some heat.
- Ⓒ As the core's heat accelerates, the outer gases begin to cool.
- Ⓓ The gases of the outer layers extend outward and heat quickly.

⁴ ➜ Giant and supergiant stars are examples of some of the oldest and largest stars discovered. Most continue to expand and are between ten to one hundred times larger than the diameter of the sun. Furthermore, their heat is more intense than the younger yellow dwarfs as it typically reaches between 2,500 to 3,500 degrees Celsius. There are three general subcategories of giant stars: blue giants, red giants, and supergiants. Blue giants are the most extreme on the heat scale of any star, and supergiants, while quite rare, are the largest known stars with some being as enormous as an entire solar system. Ultimately, most common stars pass through the red giant stage in their evolution as their hydrogen fuel source becomes depleted in their helium core's outer shell. In turn, the core begins to heat up rapidly, causing the outer layers of the shell's gases to expand outwardly and to cool to some degree. Internally, the pressure becomes relieved, and the drop in temperature gives the star its characteristic red hue.

16 Which of the following can be inferred from paragraph 4 about giant and supergiant stars?

Ⓐ They often appear in newly created galaxies.
Ⓑ There are four different categories of giants and supergiants.
Ⓒ It is possible that larger stars exist in the universe.
Ⓓ They radiate a more intense heat than do red giant stars.

17 According to paragraph 4, which of the following is true of red giant stars?

Ⓐ They are the biggest and scarcest type of star in the universe.
Ⓑ Their color derives from a reduction in heat outside the core.
Ⓒ Their inner core is mainly composed of hydrogen and other gases.
Ⓓ They are capable of becoming as vast as an entire solar system.

5 → Not all stars pass through identical stages as the others. The evolution of each star is dependent on numerous factors, including its specific gaseous makeup and the gravitational forces affecting it. The birth-mass of the star is another crucial factor in a star's development. The greater a star's mass, the more quickly it is able to fuse hydrogen into helium. Moreover, increased helium production can cause the core of the star to contract further as it, in essence, feeds more and more on hydrogen. Once completely depleted of hydrogen, a red giant's core of helium begins to combust, or burn, causing major instability with the inner core and the outer portions of the star and releasing most of its shells of gaseous energy into the surrounding region again as a nebula. Still, at its center are the remnants of the star, essentially the core itself, called a white dwarf, which is one of the final stages of a main sequence star's evolution.

18. According to paragraph 5, red giant stars become white dwarf stars because

   Ⓐ the helium burn of the inner core releases the outer gases of the star
   Ⓑ hydrogen replaces helium at the core and explodes and creates a nebula
   Ⓒ after the core of the red giant fragments, the core is essentially dead
   Ⓓ only a skeleton of the red giant remains after a nebula absorbs it

Main sequence stars are relatively young and small. The majority of known stars are main sequence stars as they account for about 85% of all stars. Additionally, their brightness, or illumination, compared to late-stage stars is not as great or intense. They rely on nuclear fission for energy by converting hydrogen, their main source of fuel, into helium. ■ Earth's own sun is a prime example of a main sequence star, which can be classified further depending on the star's special characteristics. ■ The sun is considered a yellow dwarf star due to its age, size, and, of course, color. ■ According to scientists, the sun is about 4.5 billion years old and has so far utilized half of the hydrogen fuel at its core. ■

20 Directions: Complete the table below to summarize the information about stars as discussed in the passage. Match the appropriate statements to the type of star with which they are associated. TWO answer choices will NOT be used. **This question is worth 3 points.**

Drag your answer choices to the spaces where they belong.
To remove an answer choice, click on it. To review the passage, click on **View Text**.

Answer Choices

1. Belongs to the family of giant or supergiant stars
2. Has used up about half of its fuel at this point in its life
3. Is the largest type known in the entire universe
4. Begins to cool in the outer areas away from its core
5. Relies on neighboring nebulae for gravitational force
6. Comprises the greatest number of stars known to man
7. Has a core that will eventually contract and cause imbalance

Yellow Dwarf
-
-

Red Giant
-
-
-

How to Master Skills for the TOEFL® iBT

Second Edition

Actual Test

Answers & Explanations

READING 2

DARAKWON

Actual Test
READING 2

Answers & Explanations

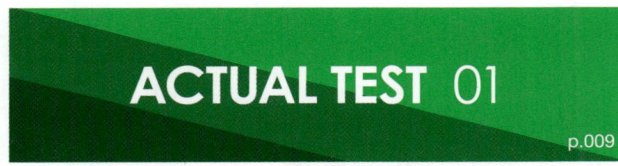

p.009

Answers

Passage 1
1 Ⓒ 2 Ⓐ 3 Ⓑ 4 Ⓒ 5 Ⓐ
6 Ⓓ 7 Ⓑ 8 Ⓒ 9 ■1
10 ②, ④, ⑥

Passage 2
11 Ⓒ 12 Ⓐ 13 Ⓓ 14 Ⓐ, Ⓑ
15 Ⓑ 16 Ⓑ 17 Ⓓ 18 Ⓐ 19 ■4
20 ②, ③, ⑤

Explanations

Passage 1 p.011

1 Vocabulary Question

Ⓒ When the climate is not static, it is not fixed but can change.

2 Rhetorical Purpose Question

Ⓐ The professor focuses on a time when the Earth's climate changed from warm to cold in writing, "Yet even during this extensive period of time, there have been warm periods interspersed with cool times. For instance, the Medieval Warm Period lasted from roughly 900 to 1300 and was promptly followed by the Little Ice Age, which started around 1300 and did not conclude until around 1850."

3 Factual Information Question

Ⓑ It is written, "The Little Ice Age was a more regional event taking place primarily in the Northern Hemisphere, particularly in Europe and North America. In Europe, glaciers rapidly expanded, causing the destruction of mountain villages in the Alps. The River Thames in England froze so solidly that people could ice skate on it in winter."

4 Inference Question

Ⓒ In writing, "There were two periods during the Little Ice Age that featured low sunspot activity. They happened from 1450 to 1540 and from 1645 to 1715. Unsurprisingly, these two periods were some of the coolest times of the Little Ice Age," the author implies that sunspots can directly affect how hot or cold the Earth is.

5 Negative Factual Information Question

Ⓐ There is no mention in the paragraph of how solar radiation causes harm to the planet.

6 Factual Information Question

Ⓓ The passage reads, "Scientists do not think that lessened sunspot activity was the trigger initiating the Little Ice Age though. Instead, many scientists believe it was volcanic activity that prompted this period of cooling to begin."

7 Inference Question

Ⓑ The author notes, "Among these eruptions was that of Tambora, a volcano in Indonesia, which erupted in 1815 in what is the biggest recorded eruption in history. It was so powerful that the following year was known as the Year Without a Summer." It can therefore be inferred that the Year Without a Summer was one of the coldest years of the Little Ice Age.

8 Sentence Simplification Question

Ⓒ The highlighted sentence notes that disruptions to currents bringing warm water north made the weather colder for a long time. This thought is best expressed in answer choice Ⓒ.

9 Insert Text Question

■1 The sentence before the first square reads, "Starting in 1257 and continuing until around 1300, there were four violent volcanic eruptions in tropical locations." The sentence to be inserted provides additional information about one of the four violent volcanic eruptions. The two sentences therefore go well together.

10 Prose Summary Question

②, ④, ⑥ The passage notes that scientists have different theories on the cause of the Little Ice Age. This thought is best represented in answer choices ②, ④, and ⑥. Answer choices ① and ③ are minor points, so they are both incorrect. Answer choice ⑤ contains incorrect information, so it is wrong, too.

Passage 2 p.021

11 Factual Information Question

Ⓒ The passage reads, "The story of their exploration is a tale of ambition, fraud, and great heroics with men eager to be hailed as the conquerors of the poles forced to the limits of human endurance."

12 Vocabulary Question

Ⓐ Problems that are at the core of a controversy are at the center of it.

13 Negative Factual Information Question

Ⓓ The author writes, "While the South Pole sits atop a 3,000-meter ice sheet covering the landmass of Antarctica, the North Pole stands atop a constantly shifting and cracking field of ice covering the Arctic Ocean."

14 Factual Information Question

Ⓐ, Ⓑ It is written, "Cook's claim was not backed up by accurate navigation records, which he said were lost. His two companions stated they had never left sight of land and had wandered for weeks, seemingly lost, meaning Cook deliberately committed fraud."

15 Sentence Simplification Question

Ⓑ The highlighted sentence points out that Scott's team could not locate its supplies and continue whereas Amundsen's team returned to its base camp. This thought is best expressed in answer choice Ⓑ.

16 Factual Information Question

Ⓑ The author points out the advantages the Norwegians had to show why they were able to reach the South Pole first.

17 Inference Question

Ⓓ The author writes, "Scott's team, weakened by injuries and illness, stalled eleven miles from a supply point and could not continue. By the end of March 1912, they were all dead. It was later asserted that faulty navigation had placed the supply point thirty miles north of where it should have been." The author therefore implies that Scott's team could have survived if they had placed the supply point properly.

18 Inference Question

Ⓐ The author writes, "One only needs to point to navigation as the key to both explorations, and in this regard, Amundsen was the master of the others. He took great pains to make sure his progress was accurate and recorded everything." It can therefore be inferred that Amundsen's navigation records confirmed that he had reached the South Pole first.

19 Insert Text Question

■4 The sentence before the fourth black square reads, "His two companions stated they had never left sight of land and had wandered for weeks, seemingly lost, meaning Cook deliberately committed fraud." The sentence to be inserted is also about fraud, so the two sentences go well together.

20 Prose Summary Question

②, ③, ⑤ The passage points out that there were several teams trying to reach the two poles first. This thought is best expressed in answer choices ②, ③, and ⑤. Answer choice ① has wrong information, so it is incorrect. Answer choices ④ and ⑥ are minor points, so they are wrong, too.

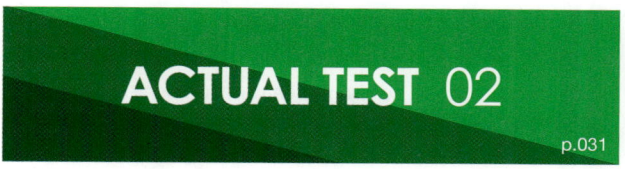

ACTUAL TEST 02

p.031

Answers

Passage 1

1 Ⓑ 2 Ⓐ 3 Ⓑ 4 Ⓓ 5 Ⓒ
6 Ⓑ 7 Ⓐ, Ⓓ 8 Ⓒ 9 ■4
10 ①, ⑤, ⑥

Passage 2

11 Ⓓ 12 Ⓑ 13 Ⓐ 14 Ⓑ 15 Ⓒ
16 Ⓐ 17 Ⓓ 18 Ⓓ 19 ■3
20 ①, ④, ⑥

Explanations

Passage 1 p.033

1 Rhetorical Purpose Question

Ⓑ The author credits telescopes for astronomers being able to create the Nebular Hypothesis in writing, "Thanks to modern technology, particularly telescopes, astronomers have come up with the Nebular Hypothesis."

2 Negative Factual Information Question

Ⓐ There is no mention in the paragraph about how large the nebula that formed Earth's solar system was.

3 Vocabulary Question

Ⓑ Variances in temperature are differences in how hot or cold something is.

4 Inference Question

Ⓓ In writing, "Rocky and metallic materials condense at higher temperatures, so they tended to be closer to the sun," the author implies that the planets close to the sun are comprised largely of rock material and metal.

5 Factual Information Question

Ⓒ The passage reads, "Rocky and metallic materials condense at higher temperatures, so they tended to be closer to the sun. On the other hand, water, methane, and other hydrogen compounds condense at lower temperatures, so they were typically farther from the sun. In addition, there was something called the frost line, which is the dividing line for different types of planets in the solar system."

6 Sentence Simplification Question

Ⓑ The highlighted sentence points out that the fact that the nebula lacked certain materials made some planets become small. This thought is best expressed in answer choice Ⓑ.

7 Factual Information Question

Ⓐ, Ⓓ The author writes, "Instead, due to cooler temperatures, the hydrogen compounds in the protoplanetary disk condensed into various ices. As more of this type of material came together, the four new planets became larger and larger. Their gravity became more powerful, which enabled them to pull in even more material, particularly hydrogen and helium in their gaseous forms."

8 Rhetorical Purpose Question

Ⓒ The author focuses on the likely creation of the Asteroid Belt in writing, "It attributes the countless asteroids in the Asteroid Belt to a fifth rocky planet that was ripped apart by the strength of Jupiter's gravity."

9 Insert Text Question

❹ The sentence before the fourth square reads, "At some point, they likely grew so large that they caused gravitational collapses, so some of the rocky material in them wound up forming the dozens of moons that orbit these planets." The sentence to be inserted focuses on the numbers of moons two planets have. The two sentences therefore go well together.

10 Prose Summary Question

❶, ❺, ❻ The passage notes that the Nebular Hypothesis describes how the planets in the solar system were formed. This thought is best expressed in answer choices ❶, ❺, and ❻. Answer choices ❷ and ❹ are minor points, so they are not right. Answer choice ❸ contains incorrect information, so it is wrong, too.

Passage 2   p.043

11 Vocabulary Question

Ⓓ Lands rife with deprivation have a lot of poverty.

12 Factual Information Question

Ⓑ The author writes, "Even in many countries with marginalized economies, there is enough food for all. It is just unevenly distributed with a powerful elite living lives of luxury in lands rife with deprivation and starvation."

13 Sentence Simplification Question

Ⓐ The highlighted passage points out that the lack of food in an area meant that large groups could not exist. This point is best expressed in sentence Ⓐ.

14 Negative Factual Information Question

Ⓑ There is no mention of how humans first managed to grow crops in the passage.

15 Factual Information Question

Ⓒ It is written, "All five independently developed agriculture from the plant species available in their regions."

16 Inference Question

Ⓐ The author writes, "With a surplus of food available, people had time to take part in activities other than food procurement. Artisans, merchants, scholars, engineers, priests, bureaucrats, permanent garrisons, and a myriad of others were fed by the surplus labor of the masses. For the first time in human history, a distinction grew between different groups of people: those who grew the food and those who did not." It can therefore be inferred that before the development of agriculture, most people were equal.

17 Vocabulary Question

Ⓓ When sins are perpetrated, they are committed.

18 Factual Information Question

Ⓓ The passage reads, "In the ancient world, cities became places of danger where crime was rife, illness spread, and the worst sins of mankind were perpetrated, a situation that remains unchanged today."

19 Insert Text Question

❸ The sentence before the third square reads, "Perversely, those who did not grow the food became more powerful by using their free time to plan cities and temples, develop weapons, gather armies, and wage war on their fellow humans." The sentence to be inserted notes that while there had been wars before agriculture, the ones that came after it and urbanization were deadlier. These two thoughts go well together.

20 Prose Summary Question

❶, ❹, ❻ The passage points out that the development of agriculture led to the urbanization of humanity. This thought is best expressed in answer choices ❶, ❹, and ❻. Answer choices ❷ and ❺ are minor points, so they are incorrect. Answer choice ❸ has information not mentioned in the passage, so it is wrong, too.

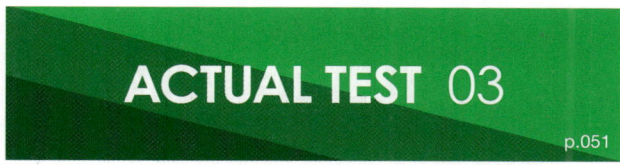

Answers

Passage 1

1. Ⓑ 2. Ⓓ 3. Ⓒ 4. Ⓒ 5. Ⓑ
6. Ⓓ 7. Ⓐ 8. Ⓑ 9. ❸
10. ①, ②, ⑥

Passage 2

11. Ⓐ 12. Ⓓ 13. Ⓒ 14. Ⓓ 15. Ⓑ
16. Ⓓ 17. Ⓑ 18. Ⓑ 19. ❹
20. ①, ②, ③

Explanations

Passage 1

1 Factual Information Question

Ⓑ The author writes, "When scientists first developed the table in the nineteenth century, they discovered that their methods of organization meant that there were some missing elements that were, as yet, unknown to man."

2 Negative Factual Information Question

Ⓓ The passage reads, "Men of knowledge in ancient Greece had proposed the atomic theory of element structure."

3 Reference Question

Ⓒ The "they" that are often placed below the table in a separate row are the rare earth elements.

4 Factual Information Question

Ⓒ It is written, "When the elements were organized according to atomic number, Mendeleev's table made more sense. Even so, it was not a perfect picture of repeated patterns."

5 Sentence Simplification Question

Ⓑ The highlighted sentence notes that the advances made in the atomic bomb project aided the search for new elements. This idea is best expressed in answer choice Ⓑ.

6 Rhetorical Purpose Question

Ⓓ The author focuses on the contributions of Glenn Seaborg to the field of chemistry in writing, "American Glenn Seaborg found it in 1940 and also had a hand in creating elements 95 to 102 in the 1940s and 1950s. He even has element 106, seaborgium, named for him, and he is responsible for much of the way the periodic table is organized today."

7 Factual Information Question

Ⓐ The author points out, "Many of these have only been created for a brief time in very specifically controlled environments, and some are presently doubted by the scientific community."

8 Vocabulary Question

Ⓑ Previously unknown elements are ones that were not known earlier.

9 Insert Text Question

❸ The sentence before the third black square reads, "It was not until the twentieth century, when new theories of atomic structure were proposed and proven, including the assigning of an atomic number based on the number of protons in an atom, that the table became more complete." The sentence to be inserted includes more information about protons. The two sentences therefore go well together.

10 Prose Summary Question

①, ②, ⑥ The passage points out that many people contributed to discoveries that led to the creation of the periodic table of the elements. This thought is best expressed in answer choices ①, ②, and ⑥. Answer choices ③, ④, and ⑤ are all minor points, so they are incorrect.

Passage 2

11 Vocabulary Question

Ⓐ When the canal was created through perseverance, it was made through determination.

12 Factual Information Question

Ⓓ The author mentions, "There were so many hardships that France, the instigator of the project, eventually had to sell out to the United States, the country that finally completed the canal."

13 Inference Question

Ⓒ First, the author writes, "One of the major reasons France abandoned the Panama Canal project was that it underestimated the environs of the local area." Then, the author notes, "However, once the Americans assumed command of the canal project, they immediately implemented better living conditions and infrastructure for the workforce, including better healthcare facilities. With a stronger workforce and a more extensive healthcare system in place, the Americans stood a better chance of completing the project than the French." It can therefore be inferred that the Americans learned from the shortcomings of the French.

14 Factual Information Question

Ⓓ The author writes, "President Theodore Roosevelt offered the Colombian government ten million dollars, which it immediately rejected."

15 Rhetorical Purpose Question

Ⓑ It is written, "Once the United States got its hands on the area, the next immediate issue was a geological obstacle. While the verdant hills of Panama looked benign enough, the diversity and makeup of the underlying sediment made it an engineering nightmare. Initially, landslides regularly destroyed weeks or even months of digging and construction as they did to the French."

16 Negative Factual Information Question

Ⓓ The author writes, "Additionally, as the tidal levels of the Pacific and Atlantic were vastly different, a new canal system, unlike the sea-level canal attempted by the French, had to be erected."

17 Sentence Simplification Question

Ⓑ The highlighted sentence notes that the project was a lofty achievement despite the high number of fatalities. This thought is best expressed in answer choice Ⓑ.

18 Factual Information Question

Ⓑ The author notes, "The canal opened endless new possibilities for trade and commerce between Asia and the Americas, which still exist today."

19 Insert Text Question

▪4▪ The sentence before the fourth black square notes, "However, once the Americans assumed command of the canal project, they immediately implemented better living conditions and infrastructure for the workforce, including better healthcare facilities." The sentence to be inserted compares the French effort regarding health care for its employees. The two sentences therefore go well together.

20 Prose Summary Question

[1], [2], [3] The passage points out that the construction of the Panama Canal was difficult but that it successfully linked the Atlantic and Pacific oceans. This thought is best expressed in answer choices [1], [2], and [3]. Answer choices [4] and [6] have wrong information, so it is incorrect. Answer choice [5] has information not mentioned in the passage, so it is wrong, too.

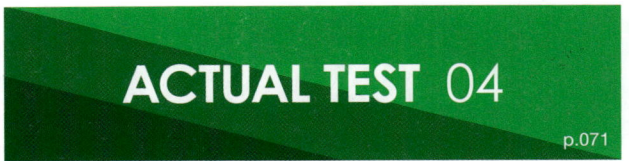

ACTUAL TEST 04

p.071

Answers

Passage 1

1 Ⓓ   2 Ⓐ   3 Ⓑ   4 Ⓐ   5 Ⓓ
6 Ⓑ   7 Ⓓ   8 Ⓐ   9 ▪4▪
10 [2], [3], [5]

Passage 2

11 Ⓒ   12 Ⓐ   13 Ⓑ   14 Ⓓ   15 Ⓑ
16 Ⓑ   17 Ⓓ   18 Ⓐ   19 ▪3▪
20 [2], [3], [6]

Explanations

Passage 1 p.073

1 Rhetorical Purpose Question

Ⓓ The author makes a contrast in writing, "At times, a new plant or animal may be introduced to an ecosystem in which it does not normally live. This is known as an exotic species. As time passes, some exotic species begin to reproduce in their new ecosystems as they establish themselves there, at which point they become known as invasive species."

2 Vocabulary Question

Ⓐ Invasive species that are highly disruptive are troublesome.

3 Sentence Simplification Question

Ⓑ The highlighted sentence notes that invasive fish can be found in both freshwater and saltwater ecosystems. This thought is best expressed in answer choice Ⓑ.

4 Inference Question

Ⓐ The author writes, "One recent study of thousands of rivers around the world determined that there were approximately 500 species of invasive fish living in them, and the researchers believed they had not found every species of fish living where they were not supposed to be." It can therefore be inferred that there are more than 500 invasive fish species in the planet's rivers.

5 Factual Information Question

Ⓓ It is written, "One of the problems with invasive fish is that they frequently have no natural predators in their new ecosystems, which makes it easy for them to reproduce and quickly to increase their numbers. As a result, they often begin outcompeting the native fish for valuable food resources. This, in turn, can cause the numbers of native fish to decline, which frequently upsets the balance in various ecosystems."

6 Negative Factual Information Question

Ⓑ There is no mention in the paragraph of how lionfish venom affects humans.

7 Reference Question

Ⓓ The "they" that feature a diversity of life are coral reefs.

8 Factual Information Question

Ⓐ The author writes, "Fishermen who catch snakeheads are urged not to release them but to kill them and to alert authorities regarding where they were caught. Likewise, scuba divers are asked to catch or kill lionfish."

9 Insert Text Question

④ The sentence before the fourth square reads, "Invasive fish such as snakeheads can therefore reduce the amount of biological diversity in some places." The sentence to be inserted provides an example of how the biological diversity in a pond can be reduced. The two sentences therefore go well together.

10 Prose Summary Question

②, ③, ⑤ The passage notes that invasive fish are problems for people and animals around the world. This thought is best expressed in answer choices ②, ③, and ⑤. Answer choices ① and ④ are minor points, so they are incorrect. Answer choice ⑥ has information not mentioned in the passage, so it is incorrect, too.

Passage 2   p.082

11 Vocabulary Question

Ⓒ When Japan was secluded from the outside world, it was isolated.

12 Negative Factual Information Question

Ⓐ The author writes, "With the exception of one Dutch ship per year at the port of Nagasaki, the Japanese refused to deal with foreign ships or nations."

13 Inference Question

Ⓑ The author notes, "Guns were imported as part of this trade, and they were one of the reasons for a great upheaval that engulfed Japan for many decades as a civil war raged between powerful shoguns, or warlords," and then adds, "Soon after the civil war, the Japanese abandoned the use of guns and the art of gun making." It can therefore be inferred that guns were blamed for the long civil war, so the Japanese stopped making them.

14 Factual Information Question

Ⓓ The passage notes, "In addition to the three main items, the Japanese agreed to allow an American consulate to be established. At first, only Nagasaki was open to American trade, but the treaty stipulated that, after five years, other ports would be opened."

15 Factual Information Question

Ⓑ The author writes, "This time, under threat of naval bombardment, the Japanese relented and finally signed the Treaty of Kanagawa on March 31, 1854."

16 Rhetorical Purpose Question

Ⓑ The author writes, "The Emperor Meiji, not wanting Japan to be under the heel of the foreigners who now clamored at the open door for pieces of his land, then set a clear path for his nation. Meiji sent sailors to England to learn how to build ships and to fight a modern naval war, invited German army officers to train his soldiers, and made deals with many companies to modernize Japan's industry, transportation, and communications."

17 Sentence Simplification Question

Ⓓ The highlighted sentence notes that the Russian defeat was surprising since Europeans usually defeated non-Europeans in wars. This thought is best expressed in answer choice Ⓓ.

18 Vocabulary Question

Ⓐ Foreign domination refers to foreign control.

19 Insert Text Question

③ The sentence before the third black square reads, "This was a precursor to the fall of the Tokugawa shoguns and the return of the emperor as the leader of Japanese affairs in 1868." The sentence to be inserted discusses the change in rulers and mentions the civil war that took place then. The two sentences therefore go well together.

20 Prose Summary Question

②, ③, ⑥ The passage points out that there were several consequences to Japan being opened in 1854. This thought is best expressed in answer choices ②, ③, and ⑥. Answer choices ①, ④, and ⑤ are all minor points, so they are incorrect.

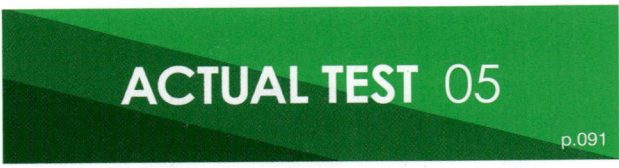

ACTUAL TEST 05

p.091

Answers

Passage 1

1 Ⓑ 2 Ⓓ 3 Ⓐ 4 Ⓒ 5 Ⓒ
6 Ⓐ 7 Ⓒ 8 Ⓐ 9 ▣4
10 ②, ④, ⑥

Passage 2

11 Ⓓ 12 Ⓐ 13 Ⓐ 14 Ⓑ 15 Ⓓ
16 Ⓒ 17 Ⓑ 18 Ⓑ 19 ▣2
20 ③, ⑤, ⑥

Explanations

Passage 1
p.093

1 Vocabulary Question

Ⓑ When skyscrapers are ubiquitous, they are pervasive.

2 Factual Information Question

Ⓓ The author writes, "The United Arab Emirates currently holds the record with Burj Khalifa standing 2,717 feet tall, but this will surely be broken at some future date as buildings are constructed ever higher."

3 Reference Question

Ⓐ The author names some building materials and then explains why buildings using them could not be very high.

4 Sentence Simplification Question

Ⓒ The highlighted sentence notes that the Bessemer process was used globally until the 1960s. This thought is best expressed in answer choice Ⓒ.

5 Factual Information Question

Ⓒ The author writes, "The secret to finding the right balance between carbon and iron to make the best steel was a quest that occupied many minds in many countries over the centuries."

6 Inference Question

Ⓐ The author notes, "Steel has also found usefulness in reinforced concrete, which is a major building material for buildings, bridges, tunnels, and countless other structures." It can therefore be inferred that steel is used in reinforced concrete.

7 Negative Factual Information Question

Ⓒ There is no mention of different ways to make steel appear more beautiful being a hindrance to making buildings higher.

8 Inference Question

Ⓐ In writing, "Historians consider the Home Insurance Building in Chicago the world's first skyscraper. It was built to ten stories in 1884-85. Although shorter than some masonry buildings, it was the first to use an all-steel frame construction to bear the weight of the floors," the author implies that the first skyscraper was not the world's highest building at that time.

9 Insert Text Question

▣4 The sentence before the fourth black square reads, "No one wants to walk up dozens of floors, so the development of the safety elevator by Elisha Otis in 1857 was a big step toward higher buildings." The sentence to be inserted mentions Otis's device as well. The two sentences therefore go well together.

10 Prose Summary Question

②, ④, ⑥ The passage notes that building height was limited before the nineteenth century but that technological developments let people make skyscrapers. This thought is best expressed in answer choices ②, ④, and ⑥. Answer choices ①, ③, and ⑤ are minor points, so they are all incorrect.

Passage 2
p.102

11 Factual Information Question

Ⓓ The author writes, "Religion and science have often clashed in this search with many people willing to believe that a higher being moves the heavens and Earth while others have looked for a physical explanation."

12 Rhetorical Purpose Question

Ⓓ The author explains why Copernicus's ideas were accepted in writing, "Copernicus was fortunate to live in the late fifteenth and early sixteenth centuries, when man was questioning his place in the universe. Then, a revolution in thinking that would be termed the Renaissance by later generations was taking place. It was not for the fainthearted, for it was dangerous to question religious fate and the creation theory of man's and the universe's existence."

13 Negative Factual Information Question

Ⓐ There is no mention in the passage that Ptolemy's theory was scientifically proven by mathematics.

14 Vocabulary Question

Ⓑ A person with considerable analytical skills has substantial skills.

15 Negative Factual Information Question

Ⓓ It is written, "Copernicus was not the first to suggest a heliocentric, or sun-centered, theory of the universe, but his is the most widely known."

16 Factual Information Question

Ⓒ The passage notes, "Copernicus, fearful of a religious backlash, kept most of his observations between himself and his assistants."

17 Sentence Simplification Question

Ⓑ The highlighted sentence notes that Copernicus made some mistakes because he did not understand gravity. This thought is best expressed in answer choice Ⓑ.

18 Inference Question

Ⓑ The author writes, "It has even been suggested that the publication of Copernicus's work enflamed the minds of Europe's greatest scientists and was the beginning of the path that led to Kepler, Newton, and Galileo." It can therefore be inferred that Galileo, Kepler, and Newton read Copernicus's famous work.

19 Insert Text Question

2 The sentence before the second black square reads, "The development of the telescope by Galileo and his observations of the planets were further proof of Copernicus's theories." The sentence to be added provides the results of Galileo's observations. The two sentences therefore go well together.

20 Prose Summary Question

3, 5, 6 The passage points out that there have been a lot of theories on Earth's position in the universe. This thought is best expressed in answer choices 3, 5, and 6. Answer choices 1 and 4 are minor points, so they are incorrect. Answer choice 2 has information not mentioned in the passage, so it is wrong, too.

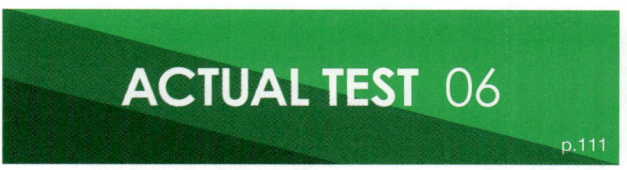

ACTUAL TEST 06

Answers

Passage 1

1 Ⓒ	2 Ⓑ	3 Ⓐ	4 Ⓑ	5 Ⓒ
6 Ⓒ	7 Ⓒ	8 Ⓑ	9 2	
10 3, 4, 6				

Passage 2

11 Ⓑ	12 Ⓐ	13 Ⓒ	14 Ⓒ	15 Ⓓ
16 Ⓐ	17 Ⓐ	18 Ⓒ	19 2	
20 2, 4, 5				

Explanations

Passage 1

1 Factual Information Question

Ⓒ It is written, "The gifted inventor recognized a need to produce cotton more quickly and devised a simple machine to solve that need. Cotton bulbs were cranked through teethed cylinders to remove the stubborn seeds lodged inside the fibrous cotton flowers."

2 Rhetorical Purpose Question

Ⓑ The author contrasts how easy it is to work with both kinds of cotton in the paragraph.

3 Sentence Simplification Question

Ⓐ The highlighted passage notes that long staple cotton was grown near the coast and that farmers needed to grow cotton farther inland to make more of it. This thought is best expressed in answer choice Ⓐ.

4 Inference Question

Ⓑ The author notes, "Long staple cotton thrived in the coastal regions mainly due to the nutrient-rich soil and the fact that its seeds were easily extracted from the cotton fibers; however, land was limited on the coast, and the need to expand inland became vital to furthering the cotton crop industry. Plantation owners quickly discovered that only the short staple variety of cotton could thrive inland, and while it was easily grown, short staple cotton provided a new complication: its sticky seeds." It can therefore be inferred that long staple cotton could not grow well away from the coastal region.

5 Inference Question

Ⓒ The author notes, "Because of its profitability, more and more land was razed with complete disregard for other natural resources, such as forests, to accommodate cotton plantations." It can therefore be inferred that cotton was considered more valuable than timber.

6 Factual Information Question

Ⓒ The passage reads, "While the cotton gin did revolutionize cotton production by removing the seeds easily and making it more efficient, the cotton bulbs themselves still had to be handpicked from the cotton plants. This led to a spike in the need for field workers, which plantation owners filled with more and more slaves."

7 Vocabulary Question

Ⓒ A multifaceted influence is one that is versatile.

8 Factual Information Question

Ⓑ It is written, "He also could not have predicted how little he himself would benefit from it even after it revolutionized the cotton industry. Because of the loose patent laws of the time as well as its simple design, the cotton gin was easily and legally replicated by others."

9 Insert Text Question

② The sentence before the second black square reads, "More than the tobacco and sugar crops grown before it, cotton, by virtue of Whitney's cotton gin, contributed to the increase in slavery in the United States." The sentence to be inserted notes that the cotton gin had an indirect effect on slavery at the time. The two sentences therefore go well together.

10 Prose Summary Question

③, ④, ⑥ The passage notes that the cotton gin helped the American economy while having negative social effects. This thought is best expressed in answer choices ③, ④, and ⑥. Answer choice ① contains information not mentioned in the passage, so it is incorrect. Answer choices ② and ⑤ are minor points, so they are incorrect, too.

Passage 2 p.123

11 Factual Information Question

Ⓑ The author notes, "Even babies have an uncanny ability to recognize music and know when it is out of tune or a false note is played."

12 Negative Factual Information Question

Ⓐ There is no mention of the making of the first musical instruments being an origin of music.

13 Sentence Simplification Question

Ⓒ The highlighted sentence notes that male pop musicians have many babies, which makes researchers believe music is necessary to reproduce. This thought is best expressed in answer choice Ⓒ.

14 Factual Information Question

Ⓒ The author mentions, "Using physical evidence from studies of testosterone levels in males and females after prolonged listening to music, the study discovered that males had lower testosterone levels and decreased sex drives while women had increased levels and were more assertive and aggressive and thus less attractive to males."

15 Reference Question

Ⓓ The "it" that people are listening to is music.

16 Inference Question

Ⓐ The author notes, "Music also alleviates stress by reducing the secretion of the hormone cortisol from the adrenal gland." It can therefore be inferred that cortisol causes increased stress levels.

17 Vocabulary Question

Ⓐ When music revives the human spirit, it enlivens the human spirit.

18 Factual Information Question

Ⓒ The passage reads, "Even so, music's ability to revive the human spirit, to reduce stress, and to make people feel a part of a group sets it apart from other arts."

19 Insert Text Question

② The sentence before the second black square reads, "This suggests that music is not so much learned as imprinted in people's brains while in the womb." The sentence to be inserted adds that studies recommend playing music for babies before they are even born. The two sentences therefore go well together.

20 Prose Summary Question

②, ④, ⑤ The passage notes that there is disagreement on the origin and purpose of music and that it has the power to unify and heal people. This thought is best expressed in answer choices ②, ④, and ⑤. Answer choice ① contains incorrect information, so it is wrong. Answer choices ③ and ⑥ are minor points, so they are incorrect, too.

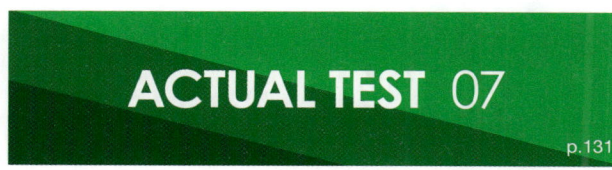

Answers

Passage 1

1 Ⓐ   2 Ⓒ   3 Ⓑ   4 Ⓒ   5 Ⓐ
6 Ⓒ   7 Ⓐ   8 Ⓓ   9 ③
10 ①, ④, ⑤

Passage 2

11 Ⓒ   12 Ⓐ   13 Ⓐ   14 Ⓒ   15 Ⓒ
16 Ⓒ   17 Ⓐ   18 Ⓑ   19 ①
20 ③, ④, ⑤

Explanations

Passage 1   p.133

1 Factual Information Question

Ⓐ The author points out, "A prime example is the Germanic tribes that were pushed west into the Roman Empire and eventually contributed to its collapse."

2 Negative Factual Information Question

Ⓒ There is no mention in the paragraph of people escaping from slavery being a reason for migration.

3 Rhetorical Purpose Question

Ⓑ The author explains why many Europeans came to America in writing, "America offered many things to attract these early settlers and those that came after. Many religious sects came in the seventeenth century, a time of religious persecution in Europe."

4 Sentence Simplification Question

Ⓒ The highlighted sentence notes that since Americans cared less about class than people in other countries, a person could do anything no matter what kind of life he was born into. This thought is best expressed in answer choice Ⓒ.

5 Inference Question

Ⓐ The author writes, "All of the lands in the west were open for migration but were difficult to get to, with great distances to traverse, hostile Native Americans to deal with, and the harshness of the terrain to contend with." It can therefore be inferred that difficult environmental circumstances made few people settle in the west.

6 Vocabulary Question

Ⓒ When immigration was largely interrupted, it was stopped.

7 Factual Information Question

Ⓐ The author notes, "The nineteenth century saw an unprecedented increase in American immigration, still mostly from Europe, including massive migration from Ireland following the potato famine of that impoverished land in the late 1840s."

8 Factual Information Question

Ⓓ It is written, "The Homestead Act was designed in part to increase migration from the eastern cities, which were expanding at rapid rates as immigration increased."

9 Insert Text Question

③ The sentence before the third black square reads, "All of the lands in the west were open for migration but were difficult to get to, with great distances to traverse, hostile Native Americans to deal with, and the harshness of the terrain to contend with." The sentence to be inserted describes some of the harsh terrain in the west. The two sentences therefore go well together.

10 Prose Summary Question

①, ④, ⑤ The passage points out that people immigrated to America and moved to the west for various reasons. This thought is best expressed in answer choices ①, ④, and ⑤. Answer choices ② and ③ have information not mentioned in the passage, so they are incorrect. Answer choice ⑥ is a minor point, so it is wrong, too.

Passage 2   p.142

11 Factual Information Question

Ⓒ The author writes, "There are many noteworthy differences between these two kinds of venomous snakes. One is the type of fangs each snake employs to attack prey or to defend itself."

12 Sentence Simplification Question

Ⓐ The highlighted sentence notes that coral snakes are venomous and colorful whereas false coral snakes are colorful but lack venom. This thought is best expressed in answer choice Ⓐ.

13 Inference Question

Ⓐ The author writes, "One of its most distinguishing features is its brightly colored red, yellow, and black bands—the pattern that other species of snakes have evolved to mimic as a defense against predators." It can therefore be inferred that other species of snakes look like the coral snake.

14 Rhetorical Purpose Question

Ⓒ The author makes a contrast in writing, "However, the coral snake, unlike true vipers such as the diamondback rattlesnake, has short, small permanent fangs in its upper jaw, which permit the slow secretion of venom. Therefore, the coral snake must grasp and continue to hold on to its prey for its venom to be effective. Vipers, on the other hand, have a pair of retractable, hollow fangs of greater size than the coral snake that can inflict a bite and jet in enough venom to incapacitate their prey in a split second."

15 Factual Information Question

Ⓒ It is written, "Vipers, on the other hand, have a pair of retractable, hollow fangs of greater size than the coral snake that can inflict a bite and jet in enough venom to incapacitate their prey in a split second. This is the main reason why the diamondback rattlesnake, not the coral snake, is considered the deadliest snake in the United States."

16 Inference Question

Ⓒ The author notes, "Moreover, backup sets of fangs replace the ones that remain lodged in prey, much like the replacement system of teeth found in sharks." It can therefore be inferred that the fangs are often embedded in an animal during an attack.

17 Vocabulary Question

Ⓐ When an individual has time to retreat, that person can move back.

18 Factual Information Question

Ⓑ The author mentions, "First, because of its colorful bands, it is more easily seen than the rattlesnake, which blends in more with the colors of its habitat. The coral snake broadcasts its presence while the rattlesnake camouflages itself."

19 Insert Text Question

1 The sentence before the first black square reads, "It is a pit viper, which denotes the small heat sensors on its face used to detect warm-blooded prey such as rodents and birds." The sentence to be inserted mentions another benefit of the small heat sensors. The two sentences therefore go well together.

20 Prose Summary Question

③, ④, ⑤ The passage points out that the coral snake and the diamondback rattlesnake are two venomous snakes. This thought is best expressed in answer choices ③, ④, and ⑤. Answer choices ① and ② are minor points, so they are incorrect. Answer choice ⑥ has information not mentioned in the passage, so it is wrong, too.

ACTUAL TEST 08

p.151

Answers

Passage 1

1 Ⓐ 2 Ⓒ 3 Ⓓ 4 Ⓒ 5 Ⓑ
6 Ⓑ 7 Ⓒ 8 Ⓑ 9 ③
10 ①, ③, ⑥

Passage 2

11 Ⓑ 12 Ⓓ 13 Ⓐ 14 Ⓒ 15 Ⓐ
16 Ⓑ 17 Ⓒ 18 Ⓐ 19 ①
20 ②, ④, ⑤

Explanations

Passage 1   p.153

1 Factual Information Question

Ⓐ It is written, "They are classified as whitewater, clearwater, and blackwater rivers, and each displays elements that make it ecologically distinct from the others. Clearly, one of the main reasons they have been named as such is due to the qualities of their appearance, but there are also fundamental differences in everything from their water consistency to abundance or lack of organisms within each type of river."

2 Vocabulary Question

Ⓒ When water has a transparent nature, it is glassy in appearance.

3 Inference Question

Ⓓ The author writes, "The clearwater rivers of the Amazon region, also called bluewater rivers, are noted for their crystal-clear water and are found flowing through the rocks of the highlands and at upper elevations." It can therefore be inferred that clearwater rivers do not exist on level areas in the Amazon.

4 Negative Factual Information Question

Ⓒ The author notes, "Overall, clearwater rivers have a very high mineral content, which allows plant life as well as algae to proliferate."

5 Rhetorical Purpose Question

Ⓑ The author focuses on why whitewater rivers are not as clear as some others in writing, "Two of the main causes of their high sediment content are the natural erosion of the river basin itself as well as the deforestation of the rainforest."

6 Factual Information Question

Ⓑ It is mentioned, "As deforestation continues, soil is no longer anchored by the roots of vegetation and trees and is instead washed into the river during the heavy rains that frequent the rainforest."

7 Factual Information Question

Ⓒ The author mentions, "Blackwater rivers are the most common type in the Amazon. They exhibit a deep dark brown color due to the decomposition of leaves and vegetation in the waters. Most vegetation contains the chemical tannin, which is released into blackwater rivers as it begins to decompose."

8 Sentence Simplification Question

Ⓑ The highlighted sentence notes that after the Amazon and Rio Negro rivers combine, their ecosystems become diverse all the way to the ocean. This thought is best expressed in answer choice Ⓑ.

9 Insert Text Question

❸ The sentence before the third black square reads, "Clearly, one of the main reasons they have been named as such is due to the qualities of their appearance, but there are also fundamental differences in everything from their water consistency to abundance or lack of organisms within each type of river." The sentence to be inserted gives an example of a lack of organisms in a river. The two sentences therefore go well together.

10 Prose Summary Question

[1], [3], [6] The passage points out that the Amazon region has bluewater, whitewater, and blackwater rivers. This thought is best expressed in answer choices [1], [3], and [6]. Answer choice [2] has information not mentioned in the passage, so it is incorrect. Answer choices [4] and [5] are minor points, so they are wrong, too.

Passage 2   p.162

11 Sentence Simplification Question

Ⓑ The highlighted sentence notes that naturalists emphasized showing life as they saw it. This thought is best reflected in answer choice Ⓑ.

12 Inference Question

Ⓓ The author writes, "Crane was born to parents in the ministry and grew up in a household grounded in religious beliefs and context. Yet before long, Crane had, for the most part, rejected religion and the idea of divine intervention in favor of a more hands-on approach to the world." It can therefore be inferred that Crane and his parents had different beliefs.

13 Factual Information Question

Ⓐ It is written, "It did not come from Crane's imagination. Rather, it stemmed from his personal experience."

14 Rhetorical Purpose Question

Ⓒ The author mentions, "As Crane continues with the theme of man versus nature in *The Open Boat*, the element of pessimism, crucial to any naturalistic work, becomes quite apparent. The men are at the mercy of the storms and the seas and cannot do much to save themselves. In this sense, Crane reveals the indifference of nature and the universe in relation to the life or plight of human beings in general."

15 Factual Information Question

Ⓐ The author writes, "The situation of the shipwreck is ideal because ordinary everyday people must face an extreme situation from which it is more than likely that they will perish. Crane continually creates a mood of impending doom and the punishing nature of the universe throughout the story. Along the way, he provides little commentary on the situation, forcing readers to place themselves immediately on the boat with the men while enforcing the dark tone of the story."

16 Reference Question

Ⓑ The "they" that have some control over their fate are the individuals in the boat.

17 Vocabulary Question

Ⓒ When Crane's work shuns a sugarcoated reality, it avoids that kind of reality.

18 Factual Information Question

Ⓐ The passage reads, "Crane ultimately shows how individuals still always have the capacity to strive together to overcome hardships and disaster."

19 Insert Text Question

❶ The sentence before the first black square reads, "While in general, the individuals may seem insignificant in the grand scheme of the universe or to nature itself, Crane instills the importance of camaraderie in the story." The sentence to be inserted provides an example of the camaraderie Crane writes about in the story. The two sentences therefore go well together.

20 Prose Summary Question

[2], [4], [5] The passage notes that *The Open Boat* by Stephen Crane is a naturalist work about how ruthless nature is. This thought is best expressed in answer choices [2], [4], and [5]. Answer choice [1] has information not mentioned in the passage, so it is incorrect. Answer choice [3] has incorrect information, so it is also wrong. And answer choice [6] is a minor point, so it is incorrect.

ACTUAL TEST 09

p.171

Answers

Passage 1

1. Ⓓ   2. Ⓑ   3. Ⓒ   4. Ⓐ   5. Ⓓ
6. Ⓒ   7. Ⓑ   8. Ⓑ   9. ■4
10. ①, ②, ④

Passage 2

11. Ⓐ   12. Ⓑ   13. Ⓒ   14. Ⓓ   15. Ⓓ
16. Ⓑ   17. Ⓐ   18. Ⓑ   19. ■3
20. ②, ④, ⑥

Explanations

Passage 1
p.173

1 Vocabulary Question

Ⓓ When sailors traversed the oceans, they crossed the oceans.

2 Rhetorical Purpose Question

Ⓑ The author notes, "Additionally, because the compass gave a general or estimated position in relation to the magnetic north pole, which was always shifting, the implementation of the cross-staff in combination with the compass often helped refine a ship's position."

3 Reference Question

Ⓒ The "it" that had a numeric scale etched was the larger staff.

4 Sentence Simplification Question

Ⓐ The highlighted sentence notes that sailors figured out the height of the sun to guess their latitude, which told them how far from the equator they were. This thought is best expressed in answer choice Ⓐ.

5 Factual Information Question

Ⓓ The passage reads, "In addition, different sizes of crosspieces were incorporated depending on the ship's distance from the equator. For example, if the ship was in close proximity to the equator, a shorter piece was used because the North Star appeared closer to the horizon. As the ship moved to the north, the gap between the North Star and the horizon widened and therefore required an adjustment in the size of the crosspiece."

6 Factual Information Question

Ⓒ The author notes, "For example, if the ship was in close proximity to the equator, a shorter piece was used because the North Star appeared closer to the horizon."

7 Factual Information Question

Ⓑ It is written, "Early navigators had to look directly at the sun in order to produce an accurate measurement; this often permanently damaged their vision. In order to compensate for or to alleviate this issue, an improved version of the cross-staff, appropriately named the back-staff, was created."

8 Vocabulary Question

Ⓑ When sailors could determine their positions more precisely, they could do that more accurately.

9 Insert Text Question

■4 The sentence before the fourth black square reads, "The navigator did not have to look directly into the sun's scorching rays but could still make an accurate reading." The sentence to be inserted contrasts that action by pointing out how sailors previously got a decent measurement. The two sentences therefore go well together.

10 Prose Summary Question

①, ②, ④ The passage notes that the cross-staff and other aids let sailors determine their latitudinal positions more accurately. This thought is best expressed in answer choices ①, ②, and ④. Answer choices ③ and ⑤ contain incorrect information, so they are both wrong. Answer choice ⑥ has information that is not mentioned, so it is incorrect, too.

Passage 2
p.181

11 Vocabulary Question

Ⓐ Cell types that constitute a human body form it.

12 Factual Information Question

Ⓑ The author notes, "The new miracle of the medical world is the stem cell, a marvel of human nature in that it can become any of nearly 220 cell types that constitute the human body. It is often called a blank cell that can be programmed to become other cells."

13 Negative Factual Information Question

Ⓒ There is no mention in the passage of artificially impregnated women being mentioned as sources of stem cells.

14 Factual Information Question

Ⓓ The passage reads, "At the core of this debate is the issue of what really constitutes a human being with one side claiming a human does not exist until born from its mother while the other side declares that once egg and sperm meet, life has begun."

15 Sentence Simplification Question

Ⓓ The highlighted sentence notes that the U.S. government makes its decision on stem cell research based upon the voting public's desires. This thought is best expressed in answer choice Ⓓ.

16 Factual Information Question

Ⓑ It is written, "Many universities and research centers worry that these laws may cause their best and brightest scientists to seek appointments overseas, where stem cell research is not so controversial."

17 Vocabulary Question

Ⓐ When pain is alleviated, it is lessened.

18 Inference Question

Ⓑ The author writes, "In the end, the research will likely get done in a place that puts existing human life above that in the embryonic state. It is also highly unlikely that that place will be the United States." It can therefore be inferred that stem cell research in many countries is regarded from a scientific viewpoint rather than from a moral one.

19 Inference Question

■3 The sentence before the third black square reads, "Unfortunately, so far, the search has not unearthed any sources as perfect as human embryo stem cells." The sentence to be inserted provides an explanation for why new sources have not been found. The two sentences therefore go well together.

20 Prose Summary Question

②, ④, ⑥ The passage notes that promising stem cell research has been hindered by the American government. This thought is best expressed in answer choices ②, ④, and ⑥. Answer choice ① is a minor point, so it is incorrect. Answer choices ③ and ⑤ have information not mentioned in the passage, so they are wrong, too.

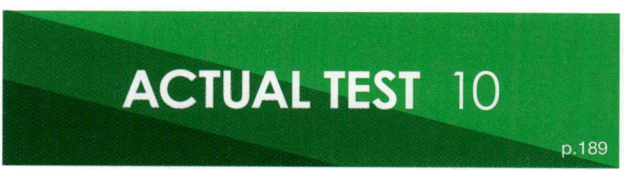

Answers

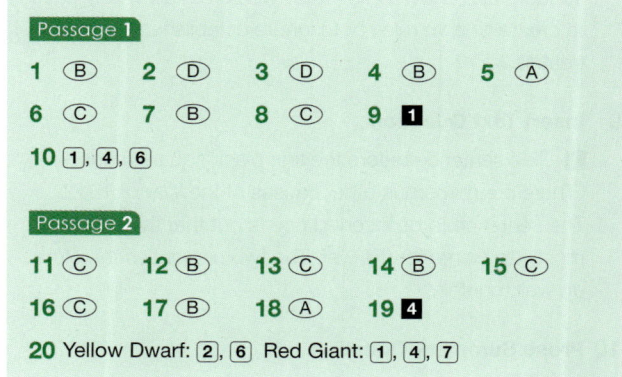

Explanations

Passage 1

1 Vocabulary Question

Ⓑ When the Americans disrupted British influence, they disturbed it.

2 Factual Information Question

Ⓓ The passage reads, "Overall, however, neither country ever really gained anything substantial."

3 Sentence Simplification Question

Ⓓ The highlighted passage notes that British actions forced the Americans to go to war. This thought is best expressed in answer choice Ⓓ.

4 Factual Information Question

Ⓑ It is written, "England continued to meddle in American commerce and treat the country much like a colony; therefore, the Americans believed the time was ripe to make a statement despite not actually expecting to defeat the entire British Empire."

5 Rhetorical Purpose Question

Ⓐ The passage notes, "Further blockades by the British allowed them to gain greater control of the oceans."

6 Inference Question

Ⓒ The author writes, "While war continued between England and France, American ships benefited by supplying the French with greatly needed supplies, which angered the British." It can therefore be inferred that the French were on better terms with the U.S. than England.

7 Negative Factual Information Question

Ⓑ The British used impressment against the Americans. The Americans did not use it against the British.

8 Factual Information Question

Ⓒ The author mentions, "The Americans also proved that they would not back down from any threats to their freedom and showed how they would not allow any country to create its own rules or to ignore established international treaties."

9 Insert Text Question

[1] The sentence before the first black square reads, "There are numerous other causes of the War of 1812." The sentence to be inserted points out that the British are mostly to blame for the war. The two sentences therefore go well together.

10 Prose Summary Question

[1], [4], [6] The passage notes that England's naval transgressions caused the United States to declare war in 1812. This thought is best expressed in answer choices [1], [4], and [6]. Answer choices [2] and [5] are minor points, so they are incorrect. Answer choice [3] has incorrect information, so it is also wrong.

Passage 2 p.199

11 Factual Information Question

Ⓒ The passage reads, "They continuously evolve and are born out of a nebula, a large mass of clouds in a galaxy."

12 Rhetorical Purpose Question

Ⓑ It is written, "Main sequence stars are relatively young and small. The majority of known stars are main sequence stars as they account for about 85% of all stars. Additionally, their brightness, or illumination, compared to late-stage stars is not as great or intense. They rely on nuclear fission for energy by converting hydrogen, their main source of fuel, into helium."

13 Negative Factual Information Question

Ⓒ The author notes, "They rely on nuclear fission for energy by converting hydrogen, their main source of fuel, into helium."

14 Vocabulary Question

Ⓑ When a star becomes sedentary, it becomes inactive.

15 Sentence Simplification Question

Ⓒ The highlighted sentence notes that a star's outer gases cool as the heat in the core increases. This thought is best expressed in answer choice Ⓒ.

16 Inference Question

Ⓒ The author mentions, "Giant and supergiant stars are examples of some of the oldest and largest stars discovered." It can therefore be inferred that stars larger than giants and supergiants may exist.

17 Factual Information Question

Ⓑ The passage reads, "Internally, the pressure becomes relieved, and the drop in temperatures gives the star its characteristic red hue."

18 Factual Information Question

Ⓐ It is written, "Once completely depleted of hydrogen, a red giant's core of helium begins to combust, or burn, causing major instability with the inner core and the outer portions of the star releasing most of its shells of gaseous energy into the surrounding region again as a nebula."

19 Insert Text Question

[4] The sentence before the fourth black square reads, "According to scientists, the sun is about 4.5 billion years old and has so far utilized half of the hydrogen fuel at its core." The sentence to be inserted notes that the sun will not run out of fuel for several billion more years. The two sentences therefore go well together.

20 Fill in a Table Question

Yellow Dwarf: [2], [6] Red Giant: [1], [4], [7]

About yellow dwarf stars, the author notes, "Main sequence stars are relatively young and small. The majority of known stars are main sequence stars as they account for about 85% of all stars," and adds, "According to scientists, the sun is about 4.5 billion years old and has so far utilized half of the hydrogen fuel at its core." As for red giant stars, the author writes, "There are three general subcategories of giant stars: blue giants, red giants, and supergiants," and adds, "Ultimately, most common stars pass through the red giant stage in their evolution as their hydrogen fuel source becomes depleted in their helium core's outer shell." The author further writes, "Once completely depleted of hydrogen, a red giant's core of helium begins to combust, or burn, causing major instability with the inner core and the outer portions of the star."

Actual Test
READING 2